Praise for *The Age of Thrivability*

"Never before – that I know of – has the impor
conveyed with such clarity and insight.

With a light-hearted tone yet depth of wisdom, Holliday articulates the way forward
to enable our organisations to move beyond the reduction of negative impact toward
full-bodied participatory engagement within life. It is truly heart-warming to read a
book that so eloquently conveys love of life in such practical ways. With insights at every
turn, she invites us to see with fresh eyes and learn to sense the wisdom within and all
around us.

The Age of Thrivability *is an important and timely contribution to a deepening conversation on how we transform our social and organisational systems into living systems
that tend toward harmony with Life. This is a must-read for those interested in our life-
affirming future.*"

Giles Hutchins, speaker, adviser and author of *Future Fit, The Illusion of Separation*
and *The Nature of Business*

"Holliday has done something I greatly admire and respect. She weaves together the
spiritual and the material, as living systems are, into useful and hopeful ways of crossing
the chasm between paradigms. Inspiring reading!"

Carol Sanford, regenerative business educator and author of *The Responsible
Business* and *The Responsible Entrepreneur*

"A comprehensive review of the background and principles behind thrivability, this book
weaves together the multiple layers, threads, stories, and metaphors of what thrivability
means and what it could become."

Finn Jackson, consultant and author of *The Escher Cycle: Building Self-Reinforcing
Business Advantage* and *The Churning: Tools for Leadership in Times of Change*

"The Age of Thrivability *is an inspirational roadmap for taking us out of our current economic, social and ecological crisis and into a new paradigm, through the exploration of multiple and divergent perspectives, the dynamic processes of natural systems and a holistic conception of the unity of life. Michelle Holliday provides us with the systemic frameworks, case studies and practical guidelines needed to shift our way of thinking towards the effective stewardship of our organisations, communities and planet."*

Simon Robinson, co-author of *Holonomics: Business Where People and Planet Matter*

"*Michelle Holliday's* The Age of Thrivability *is a field book offering leaders and facilitators history, frameworks and useful insights on how to cultivate thrivable environments in work, community and family contexts. What is even more compelling is the explicit call to action. Beyond the generous knowledge transfer, put the book down and pick up the baton. The reader is evoked to be more mindfully explicit of each interaction as a teachable moment. We are always moving to and from thrivability. May your torch shine brightly."*

Jennifer Sertl, founder of Agility3R, co-author *of Strategy, Leadership & the Soul*

"*In* The Age of Thrivability, *Michelle shows us that the innovation we desperately need in our world is not how to make* stuff *but in* humanbeing, *in patterning our lives and the lives of our organizations according to a template that was here before we arrived on the scene. The language is hopeful and the vision is rich in possibility. The practices are based on timeless principles that can be as infinitely generative in human society as they are in nature. When followed, as in nature, we all thrive together and our organizations and society will be the better for it."*

Tolu Ilesanmi, CEO, Zenith Cleaners

"In this extraordinary sweep of ideas from across the new sciences of human flour-ishing and living systems, Michelle Holliday takes us on a tour of meaning-making to help change the human story from anguish and anxiety to thriving with and as part of nature. With attention to the convergence of science and spirit, she demonstrates how human self-organization and creativity generates new living systems and collectivities that bring forth energized life, possibility and engagement. I recommend that the reader spend time with these ideas as if they could seriously intervene in the "business as usual" organizations and cultures we tend to accept without question. The Age of Thrivability shows us a powerful pathway to transformative change."

Peter Jones, PhD, Associate Professor in the Faculty of Design at OCAD University, Founder of Design with Dialogue, author of *Design for Care, We Tried to Warn You,* and *Team Design.*

"If you are looking for a read that is heady and profound, filled with truths and certainty, this book is not for you. If you are willing to let yourself be aroused, to dance with im-ages and ideas about what kind of world is possible now, then please pick up The Age of Thrivability. *Michelle Holliday is one of the few people who both understand living sys-tems conceptually AND who see and understand what those concepts mean as a lived experience in these times. The Age of Thrivability masterfully weaves together mind, body, spirit and stories in an important exploration of what is possible now."*

Bob Stilger, PhD, co-president of NewStories, former co-director of Berkana Institute, author of *AfterNow.Today: When the Future is Invisible, Where Do We Begin?*

"Michelle writes of complex things that people and organizations are tackling and she does this with an extraordinary love and clarity. She reveals a deep understanding of how we evolve and change alongside the projects and initiatives we care for and are entrusted to steward. She is a scribe to an emerging era, with a worldview and a set of practices and attitudes that are showing us a radical story of collective thrivability."

Vanessa Reid, co-founder, The Living Wholeness Institute

THE AGE OF THRIVABILITY

THE AGE OF THRIVABILITY

Vital Perspectives and Practices for a Better World

March 2024
Jon!
Amazing to be in
these conversations
with you here in Portugal.
And so happy to know about
your powerful work in the world.
Much admiration,
Michelle

MICHELLE HOLLIDAY

ISBN-13: 9780995275904
ISBN-10: 0995275904

Library and Archives Canada Cataloguing in Publication

Holliday, Michelle (Michelle Suzanne), author
    The age of thrivability : vital perspectives and practices for a better world / Michelle Holliday.

ISBN 978-0-9952759-0-4 (paperback)

    1. Environmental ethics. 2. Human ecology. 3. Sustainability.
I. Title.

GF80.H65 2016   304.2   C2016-906378-X

TABLE OF CONTENTS

Foreword by Michael Jones ·xiii

Who is this book for? · xvii

How to read this book ·xix

Section 1   **The Context and the Need**· 1

    1.1   My Story and the Story of this Book · 3

    1.2   The Broader Context and Intention of the Book · · · · · · · · · · · 9

Section 2   **Understanding the Patterns of Our Thriving**· · · · · · · · · · · · 17

    2.1   A Quick Overview · 19

    2.2   Science's Unfolding Explanation of Life · · · · · · · · · · · · · · · · · 23

    2.3   The Evolution of our Social Context· 47

    2.4   The Evolving Brain· 65

    2.5   An Emerging Level of Consciousness · · · · · · · · · · · · · · · · · · · 77

Section 3   **Committing to the Practice of Thrivability**· · · · · · · · · · · · · · 91

    3.1   Cue Thrivability · 93

    3.2   The Living Organization · 96

    3.3   Story #1: *Espace pour la vie* · 104

    3.4   The Trifocal Lens · 108

    3.5   Story #2: Zenith Cleaners · 115

    3.6   The Call to Stewardship · 119

    3.7   Story #3: CLC Montreal · 125

    3.8   Embodying All the Patterns· 129

3.9   Story #4: Experiencing Mariposa · 135
3.10   Measuring Thrivability · 140
3.11   Story #5: Crudessence · 148
3.12   The Vital Role of Death · 151

Section 4   Moving into The Age of Thrivability · 157
4.1   The Need for Practice Grounds · 159
4.2   What Becomes Possible · 166

       Resources · 169
       Acknowledgements · 171
       About the Author · 175
       Endnotes · 177

*Guided by what we know about living systems, thrivability [calls for]
a continual and purposeful drive to create the fertile conditions for
life to thrive at the levels of the individual, the organization, the community and the biosphere. Profoundly practical, it is distinguished
by a deep understanding of how life works - and by intentional
participation in that pattern. The thrivability movement recognizes
that only by aligning with life in the spirit of learning, compassion,
contribution and play can we find the motivation and the means to
collaborate and innovate at the levels required.*

MICHELLE HOLLIDAY, "THE PRACTICE OF THRIVABILITY"[1]

FOREWORD

By Michael Jones

WE ARE BETWEEN stories. The old story is no longer working for us and the new story is not quite here. To help map our way through these times of transition and ambiguity we look for guides who can articulate what cannot yet be clearly seen or understood. Through her book, *The Age of Thrivability*, Michelle Holliday serves as one of our new guides. She is both an insightful cartographer and an inspired story-teller. What she offers in this book is a broad and sweeping view of a thrivable future crafted out of stories that are filled with magic, boldness and possibility.

"There are two ways of looking at life," she writes, quoting a remark by Albert Einstein. "One as though nothing is a miracle and the other, as though everything is a miracle." And miracles appear throughout *The Age of Thrivability*. What we discover is that, not only is life a miracle itself, but there is a greater miracle, and that is that life always seeks more life.

What that means is that we are an integral part of a universe that is held together, not only through the physical principles of gravity, but through allurement and love. She writes: "There is an underlying tendency or urge in all life to connect with other life in order to create emergent, transcendent forms."

To imagine that we are part of an intelligence governed by the principles of attraction in a universe that is always seeking to become more of itself is breathtaking. We cannot return to our old ways of thinking once Michelle has awakened us to the deeper nature of the world we find ourselves in. This worldview suggests that, in the midst of life's strife and struggle, there is something at the very heart of it all – an impulse, a pattern of connection, an urge – even an urgency to embrace what Lebanese poet Khalil Gibran calls, "life's longing for itself."

This longing is an ache in the heart that runs throughout all of Michelle's writing. The ache reminds us that where there could have been nothing – an emptiness, a void, or a black hole – there is something. And this something fills the emptiness with beauty, grace and love. This is the thrivable ground she writes of. A thrivability that recognizes how the connections, patterns and characteristics in our organizations, our communities and ourselves reflect life's longing to be reunited with itself.

Michelle invites us to nourish this longing for life, because ultimately it is this longing that does all the work. And the work, as she describes it, is to be stewards of life's conscious evolution in order that life's constant pursuit of ever-higher levels of emergence and self–transcendence can be realized.

As a pianist and composer, I am familiar with how a musical composition grows in beauty and complexity – and often transcendence – each time I play. As she suggests, I cannot create this outcome directly. But I *can* create the conditions for this to happen on its own.

Out of this cultivated ground there arises a propensity or inner necessity to create. An urge that engages us with the phenomenon of *autopoiesis*, which means self-creation – the experience of life's eternal longing to experience and re-generate itself.

Crafting this new narrative for the future is what makes *The Age of Thrivability* both vital and necessary. Reading it, I am reminded of an interview between the award-winning broadcast journalist Bill Moyers and CEO and poet James Autry. Autry was among thirty-four poets that Moyers was interviewing as part of a PBS Series on *The Language of Life*. He hoped to gain a deeper understanding of the notion of autopoiesis through exploring commentaries on the lives of poets and their poetry.

During the interview, Moyers seemed puzzled as he tried to understand how Autry could cross over from celebrating his poetry at public festivals to reading it to his supervisors and staff in the competitive – and often tough-minded – world of business.

To this, Autry replied: "It's crucially important for business people to feel that what they're doing in business *is* life. There is only life, and business is part of that."

It is in this context that *The Age of Thrivability* is revolutionary. There are many books on leadership and organization that offer diverse points of view – but they share a common context, which is that life serves business. What makes this book unique is that it shifts the context to say: business serves life. And, as Michelle writes, this story has the power to change everything, including what it means to be human and alive and at work in the world.

Plato wrote:

This world is indeed a living being endowed with a soul and intelligence... a single visible living entity containing all other living entities, which by their nature are all related.

And this is Michelle's call to us. There is one single narrative – a living intelligence – that is "at once radically revolutionary and timelessly true." To align with this living intelligence is the work of the future. To manifest this in our stewardship of life is our gift to ourselves and to the world.

Michael Jones is a widely recognized leadership educator, keynote speaker, thought leader, pianist composer and storyteller. He is an award-winning author of a series of books on reimagining leadership, including: The Soul of Place, Artful Leadership *and* Creating an Imaginative Life. *He is also a Juno nominated (Canadian Grammy) pianist and composer whose 16 popular recordings of original piano music have served as a benchmark for contemporary instrumental music and attracted an audience of millions worldwide.*

WHO IS THIS BOOK FOR?

THIS BOOK DOESN'T easily fit into one category. "Management literature" is too small (and not quite accurate). "Philosophy" doesn't cover it fully, broad as that topic may be. Indeed, *The Age of Thrivability* touches on history as well as future trends, on science as well as spirituality, and on the meaning of life as well as practical questions of how change happens within organizations.

With such a wide-ranging scope, it is intended for thoughtful, curious people who are concerned about the future of humanity. It is for readers who are interested in new stories and the patterns that connect them. It is for those who value wisdom and compassion, and who feel certain these two traits are critical for the path ahead.

In particular, it is written for people who find themselves at the intersection of organizational leadership, social innovation, and an emerging paradigm rooted in life and living systems.

No matter what the context, however, this book is for people who would be well served by insights into how life works and what those insights mean for our organizations and communities.

In other words, it is for you.

How to read this book

I F WE WERE together in conversation, I would be able to ask you about your interests and offer only the angles and anecdotes that would be most relevant for you. But unfortunately, a book doesn't afford that level of personalization. Some sections may appeal to you more than others. And so, you will have to make your own choices about what to focus on along the way, as every reader does.

There are two opening chapters that lay out the "menu," setting the scene in different ways and whetting the appetite for the new story of thrivability.

Next are several chapters that reveal the core patterns of living systems in a variety of contexts, each of which shapes our understanding of the world. I invite you to approach this section as an open buffet. Sample the topics that appeal to you most. Read until you feel well satisfied.

Then meet me again in the third section to explore how these insights might feed your work in the world. In particular, I hope you'll enjoy the sprinkling of inspiring real-life stories from people within organizations and communities that have embraced the principles of thrivability. They offer a tantalizing taste of the future that awaits us, if only we choose to align with life.

Finally, the fourth section suggests some profound – and practical – ways to move forward into the Age of Thrivability.

May you find it a truly nourishing experience along the way!

SECTION 1

THE CONTEXT AND THE NEED

1.1

MY STORY AND THE STORY OF THIS BOOK

THOUGH MUCH OF *The Age of Thrivability* is written in an objective, sometimes even academic style, there is a personal story and a human voice behind it. If you have been drawn to this book, then I suspect you'll find familiar threads in my story – not in the specific circumstances, perhaps, but in the yearnings, observations and inquiries that drove me to research and write and that continue to propel me in my work today.

This book first came to life in the lovely and elegant St-Germain-des-Prés arrondissement of Paris, where my husband and I spent a year and a half in 2001 and 2002 while he was on a temporary work assignment. As an accompanying spouse, I was not legally allowed to work, and that suited me just fine. Not only was a sabbatical in Paris a heavenly proposition, I was determined to use this time to find answers to questions that plagued me about the nature of work and life.

It was a deliciously fertile time. My days were full of beauty, possibility and an easy alignment with the rhythms of life. Curiosity was my guide, luring me into topics as wide-ranging as biology, organizational theory, architecture, anthropology, history and philosophy. For me, the city's every half-hidden courtyard, ornate doorknob and ancient cobblestone radiated inspiration, though I spent much of my time in the gardens of the Rodin Museum, the towering bronze figure of *The Thinker* joining me in deep contemplation. Overlaying all of this, my search for insights was kindled by the sense that I was responding to a powerful, important calling.

Leading up to these inspired days in Paris, I had spent the first part of my career in brand strategy, working in Moscow for two major multinational corporations. Those were exciting and revolutionary times in that part of the world, and the results we achieved broke new ground in a number of important arenas. But it was there that I grew disenchanted with the ways in which businesses engaged their customers. Though it's obvious to many, I was surprised to find corporate marketing so superficial, manipulative and really just banal. I was also disillusioned with how people worked together inside large companies, which appeared more often to be in competition than in collaboration. It seemed as if there was some important point of logic missing within the prevailing assumptions about business. But I struggled to put my finger on it. And the rest of the world seemed to think things were just fine.

The disconnect grew to the point that I became sick, with chronic abdominal pain doctors couldn't explain. And so I decided to leave both marketing and large corporations and look elsewhere for more meaningful work. I found it in a small consulting firm in Washington, DC, that helped clients improve culture, leadership and internal systems. The focus was on engaging employees, which was work I found far more rewarding (and that my "innards" found much more amenable). My colleagues and I regularly talked about purpose and passion – about engaging the human spirit – well before those concepts were in vogue. But again, my sense was that major assumptions were somehow *off*. The general request from clients seemed to be: "Just tell us what buttons to push to make our people work harder for the same amount of money." Behind this request was a belief that was articulated openly by more than one organizational leader: "There is no place for the human spirit in business." *How can that be?* I wondered in confusion. *How does that even make sense?*

I also began to notice that humanity in general seemed stuck in disastrously unsustainable patterns. According to the media, I wasn't alone: millions were recognizing this, but we couldn't imagine different ways of being. *What are we missing?* I wondered. *And is all of this somehow related?*

Then I realized (as so many have by now) that the common thread across all my observations was an overarching guiding story – the dominant Western worldview that tells us that everything in the universe operates like a machine, that we and our organizations and economies exist only to compete and consume, and that we are separate from nature and from each other. Within this mechanistic paradigm, a customer relationship is nothing more than a transactional means to maximum profit. The human spirit certainly doesn't belong. And it is perfectly appropriate for the sustainability and corporate social responsibility movements to struggle to make the business case for their efforts, even when life is in the balance.

With these observations in tow, I arrived in Paris with questions like: How did we come to see our organizations and economies as machines? If I believe there is more to the story – that there is also life inside the machine – then what do I mean by that? What does "the human spirit" really mean? And how would insightful answers to these questions be useful on a practical level? What would we *do* with such information?

My thirst for understanding led me to research biology, most of all. I needed to grasp how life works – and especially *what it takes for something that is alive to thrive*. And though every biologist offers a slightly different and usually complicated explanation, a core set of patterns began to emerge across all of my reading. Importantly, those patterns matched with what I was finding in my research into organizational theory – the underlying conditions needed for a living system to thrive were the same conditions needed for an organization to thrive. For me, this was a thrilling discovery!

In fact, I began to see those same conditions everywhere I looked – in virtually every discipline I studied, and even in my own life. And at first, this disturbed me tremendously! I had recently watched the brilliant Oscar-winning movie, *A Beautiful Mind*. It dramatized the life of John Nash, a Nobel prize-winning mathematician who was also schizophrenic, a condition that led him to imagine patterns in everything around him. Seeing this powerful, yet at times disconcerting, film fed into my fear that, at best, I was eagerly force-fitting the patterns into places where they didn't truly belong and, at worst, I was irrationally imagining things that weren't really there. But as the patterns' repeated presence became undeniable, I settled into the realization that it must be natural to see them everywhere if they are, in some way, the universal means for life to create itself.

Since those months of exciting discoveries in Paris, I've spent the past decade bringing these patterns of living systems into my consulting work with a range of organizations. The patterns, which I will describe in the chapters ahead, have proven to be consistently relevant and useful, helping leaders understand the conditions they must cultivate if their organizations are to thrive – that is, to support what I and others call their *thrivability*. Perhaps even more importantly, recognizing their organizations as living systems has encouraged those leaders to see themselves less as engineers and managers and more as *stewards* in service of life. This stance makes all the difference for the people and processes within the organization, releasing energy and creativity, inviting engagement, and opening up all sorts of new and highly rewarding possibilities.

Over the years, I've also presented these patterns and my perspectives on thrivability to dozens of groups and explored them in conversations with countless individuals – biologists, historians, philosophers, economists, physicists, artists, organizational scholars, seasoned consultants, MBA students, and many others. Those exchanges have added texture to my understanding of the patterns and confirmed my belief that there is something broadly relevant and truly important in them.

Along the way, and quite apart from my own efforts, the world has gradually become more aware of living systems principles. The vocabulary of emergence, resilience and self-organization has grown more common, as has the general language of purpose, passion and thriving. Even the human spirit has emerged as a more welcome concept.

It has also been more widely acknowledged that we are moving out of a mechanistic paradigm and into one characterized by adaptability, interrelatedness and creativity (characterized by *life*, I would say).

So what's still missing? Why offer this book to the world?

Well, in my experience, the "machine story" is still going strong, especially among organizational and political leaders. It's one thing to use new vocabulary; it's another to understand what's really behind it. And it's still another to embrace it as the full nature of reality – and as the nature of *your* reality as a leader, a community member, and a human being. From what I can see, there's still a pervasive need for clear, guiding insight into what leads to thrivability, why that's important, and what it might mean to each of us.

On a larger scale, I believe the shift described in this book is what's needed – more than ever – if humanity is going to make it through the myriad and pressing global problems we're collectively facing. Far more of us need to be acutely aware that there is life within and around us in our organizations, communities and beyond. Far greater numbers of us need to feel a sense of reverence, service and profound participation in life's unfolding. Many more of us must listen deeply for what's needed and respond with wise action. Organizations can be perfect practice grounds for this, but the applications and implications are both personal and universal.

As you read, please know that I offer this book not as a complete and final proclamation of Truth but as an invitation into reflection, conversation and shared exploration. Although this book has been exhaustively researched, and although I consider myself a worldly, well-traveled person, there will inevitably be cultural gaps in the perspectives described. My lens is inescapably North American. And still, I have faith that you will find something of relevance and value in these pages.

In all, my hope is that this book will leave you feeling at least one, if not all, of the following:

- affirmed, as you find that these pages have put into words and given detail to something you've sensed, perhaps without being able to articulate it fully;
- pleasantly challenged by some new concepts and connections, even as you recognize many things you already knew;

- a rekindled love of life, including a renewed sense of wonder and gratitude;
- inspired, as you see the patterns of living systems all around you, too, and as this insight suggests ways to nurture the life in your own family, organization and community; and,
- hopeful that humanity may ultimately find its way to thriving.

These have certainly been my feelings in writing this book.

Thank you for joining me on this journey.

Michelle Holliday
Montreal, Quebec

1.2

The Broader Context and Intention of the Book

W E SEEM TO be a planet on the verge of a nervous breakdown. Ecosystem degradation threatens the survival of our species and extinguishes countless others on a daily basis. Poverty, violence and social tension persist tenaciously. And global economies are at their most vulnerable since the Great Depression.

The sustainability, corporate social responsibility and related movements have long been our best hope for pulling back from the brink and establishing new, vital practices and healthy patterns of living. And they do a tremendous amount of good. But it's becoming increasingly clear that something more is needed. Too often mired in the incremental, those movements are not getting us where we need to go – not far enough, not fast enough. And they're not satisfying a deep hunger that many of us harbor.

The premise of this book is that existing efforts don't need to be abandoned; they just need to be positioned within a larger context. We need an expanded story to be able to see what else is possible beyond our current habits of thought and action.

The good news is that such an expanded story is readily available – and already spreading. In fact, the following chapters present evidence that this emerging narrative is the natural and obvious next stage in human evolution.

At the heart of this story is an understanding of the core characteristics of thriving living systems – of what's needed for life to thrive. The story also recognizes those characteristics within our organizations, our communities, our economies – and, in fact, across all of human civilization. And with these insights, the expanded story ushers in a shift in the purpose of all our activities, toward what some are calling *thrivability* – the intention and practice of enabling life to thrive as fully as possible, at every level.

This emerging thrivability movement is more momentous than it may appear. Enabling life to thrive is not currently the explicit and primary intention in most spheres of human activity. Instead, we generally set our sights on lesser goals – and, as a result, we are getting something substantially *less* than thriving.

However, as we see how much "non-thriving" is happening in the world, what if we explore what thriving would look like – and what it would require?

Given the rising popularity of organizational practices promising agility, resilience, emergence, self-organization – living systems concepts, all of them – what if we went to the root of these practices and deeply understood how living systems work? And what if that understanding were somehow simple and useful, opening up new insights and suggesting new ways forward?

As we recognize the patterns and characteristics of life within our organizations and communities, what if we made it our primary intention and goal to enable life to thrive within them as fully as possible?

Perhaps at the heart of it all, what if our most powerful role, both individually and collectively, is to act as stewards of life's processes, actively cultivating the fertile conditions for life to thrive? And what if acting in accordance with this "prime directive" helped us achieve all of our other objectives more effectively?

These questions are at the heart of what some are calling "The Great Transition,"* as humanity moves into a new worldview that is both more complete and more useful.

In fact, this so-called "new story" has always been available. After all, it's the story of how life works – of how living systems create and sustain themselves. And if we know what to look for, we can find guidance from the simple set of patterns that's common to every form of life, at any level of complexity. It's present in sea sponges, ant colonies, rainforests and our bodies. It's how our brains operate and how effective organizations function. It shapes our very consciousness. And it's what has guided the evolution of our species over the ages. If a living system is to thrive, it must have the handful of characteristics described in the following chapters. And if we are to be wise stewards, *it is these conditions we must tend.*

Even as this story is both simple and as old as life itself, though, our newfound awareness of it has the power to change everything, including what it means to be human, and alive, and at work in the world. This awareness can help us grasp a new logic that is at once radically revolutionary and timelessly true, bringing together people and planet into a single narrative, not in conflict with each other or even in awkward conciliation, but in natural alignment. It brings to light an ethos and a set of principles that – at long last – give us permission to do what really needs to be done, making it sensible to do what our hearts often know to be the right thing in our own lives, in our organizations, and in our communities.

To bring that better future for all into clearer focus, **Section Two** offers a brief overview of the core patterns of living systems. It then dives more deeply into them, offering a whirlwind tour of several disciplines:

Chapter 2.2 reviews science's evolving explanation of life, from a clockwork universe to a systems perspective to a living systems view.

---

* First introduced by the Global Scenario Group, an international, interdisciplinary body convened in 1995.

Chapter 2.3 reveals the characteristics of living systems in the evolutionary path of humanity, charting how we developed in specific ways in each past era and how the current age calls for (and in many ways already demonstrates) newfound integration of all those perspectives and capabilities.

Chapter 2.4 shows the patterns of living systems in the way the human brain works, suggesting ways we can unleash even more intellectual power to solve our most challenging problems.

Chapter 2.5 delves into our individual consciousness, showing how each of us moves toward maturity along the familiar patterns of life and highlighting the characteristics of wisdom that are urgently required.

Together, these four domains (science's explanation of life, our social context, the workings of the brain, and individual consciousness) strongly shape how we understand and engage with the world. In each of them, the core patterns of living systems are evident, pointing to the emergence of an important new epistemology (way of knowing). And in each, there is a clear trajectory toward a promising new epoch in human evolution, if only we align with life's guiding principles in time to avert catastrophe.

Section Three then offers a series of reflections on the implications of the living systems lens, particularly for our organizations and communities. The disastrous system-level characteristics of ecosystem degradation, poverty and economic fragility are not the fault of any one of us. They emerge from patterns of collective action. For the most part, it's not what any *one* of us does that is problematic – it's what whole crowds of us do *together* that shapes the world. And so the collective realms of our lives are where we most need to bring this new story of life *to life*. To these ends, Section Three shines a light on an emerging ontology (way of being), adding useful detail to the view of organizations as living systems and offering guidance about the perspectives that are needed to steward life within them.

Finally, **Section Four** invites us into the ongoing practice of cultivating thrivability in our daily lives.

These chapters and the stories that accompany them demonstrate that when we truly acknowledge the life in and around us and our ability to create the conditions for life to thrive, new visions of reality become apparent: new possibilities, new goals, new priorities and new actions. In embracing the perspectives this story of thrivability offers, we become more active and intentional participants in life's process. And along the way, we find a path to richer meaning, to greater compassion, to more effective collaboration, to healthy regeneration and renewal, and to more thriving, in all senses of the word.

Ultimately, if we are to navigate increasing complexity successfully... if we are to bridge the many fragmented approaches to sustainability and corporate social responsibility... if we are to solve the persistent problems of poverty, environmental degradation and conflict... and, indeed, if our species is to survive, it is precisely such an expanded lens and inspired approach that is needed.

All of this may sound naively utopian, denying the world we see before us today and the fundamental aspects of human nature that have contributed to the problems we face – things like competition for scarce resources and individual self-interest. But the lens of thrivability doesn't deny those aspects. It *defies* them, in the grand tradition of Daniel Bernoulli.

A Swiss mathematician and physical scientist, Bernoulli is most famous for his eighteenth-century discovery of the principle that paved the way for human flight. His principle illustrated that air moving faster over the top of a shaped wing will have lower pressure than air moving more slowly underneath the wing. This difference in pressure will cause graceful lift – and flight. But his more important contribution may have been to set a precedent for going beyond the previously accepted laws and limitations of science. He didn't dispute the existence or validity of the law of gravity. Instead, he discovered a principle that allowed people to transcend it – both figuratively and literally.

Until Bernoulli's principle was applied to early planes, intrepid inventors modeled their various attempts at aircraft after the dynamics of birds – the only known model for flight. These flapping contraptions did succeed in getting off the ground, but not far and not for long. Spurred on by their limited success, their designers continued to focus on incremental improvements to their model, all to no greater success.*

Then came a brilliant flash of insight: instead of working so furiously and gracelessly against gravity, why not use another force of nature to *transcend* it? Wings were affixed firmly to the sides of the plane and designed to direct air over them faster than it could travel under them. Speed was applied, and *voila!* Takeoff! What followed was a blindingly rapid series of advancements that led to modern jet airplanes and space travel. So potent was this transcendent principle that we put a man on the moon a mere *sixty years* after Wilbur and Orville made their first hesitant flight.

Similarly, thrivability rises above the piecemeal, incremental efforts and compromises of sustainability and corporate social responsibility, offering nothing less than a soaring path out of the desperate race in which humanity seems to be caught. The unseen force with the power to provide graceful lift is life itself. And in our organizations and communities, that dynamic force may be thought of as the human spirit – the part of each of us that is vital and alive, passionate and creative, ever seeking opportunities for connection and contribution.

Taking advantage of this transcendent principle calls for stretching our perceptions beyond the current Western guiding story. It requires looking beyond familiar "flapping" tactics to entirely new perspectives. And it means shifting from a reductionist, mechanistic understanding of reality to an integral, organic paradigm. As with Bernoulli's important insight, this calls for imagination and more than a little faith.

Yet there is considerable incentive to move ahead. Our ecology, our economic systems and our social structures together rely on our ability to move toward more life-enhancing ways of acting in the world. And though there are signposts pointing the way to a hopeful future, it's far from clear that we'll actually get there. The Mayans and the ancient Greeks offer fair warning that collapse and regression are always possible.

---

* To be fair, there is still today an active Ornithopter Society dedicated to achieving flight in this way. They have had notable success with small craft the size of birds.

The more of us who embrace and begin living out the emerging story now, the more likely we all are to reach the destination that calls to us from the horizon.

For individual readers, the insights contained in this book will:

- help you understand what to bring forward from the previous story;
- lay out a simple but powerful blueprint for how to thrive in the story we're moving into;
- give you confidence to challenge assumptions, as well as courage to try new, more effective practices.

In these ways and more, *The Age of Thrivability* offers important shifts in understanding and practical ways to act on these shifts. It also gives an important glimpse into the wisdom, joy and compassion for all life that are at the heart of the dawning era. None of these values featured prominently in the guiding story of the Industrial Era. But *all* will be needed in large quantities if we are to counteract the grave problems we face as a species.

At a global level, *The Age of Thrivability* offers nothing less than a revision of human history, revealing how we have unwittingly participated in life's inherent patterns throughout the ages. Now, newly aware of this, we can become active, intentional participants and bold, life-sustaining stewards.

As activist and eco-philosopher Joanna Macy says:

The most remarkable feature of this historical moment on Earth is not that we are on the way to destroying the world — we've actually been on the way for quite a while. It is that we are beginning to wake up, as from a millennia-long sleep, to a whole new relationship to our world, to ourselves and each other.[2]

SECTION 2

UNDERSTANDING THE PATTERNS OF OUR THRIVING

2.1

A QUICK OVERVIEW

LAST SUMMER, A landscape architect friend helped me plant a sizeable and varied flower garden in my yard. This year, the garden came back gloriously – along with an overwhelming crop of myriad weeds. As a novice gardener, I couldn't quite be sure which plants were welcome and which were not. So my friend came back and helped me get better acquainted with the different characteristics and needs of my charges. As we stood next to the garden after clearing the weeds, he reached out and plucked one more. It had been partly hidden alongside one of the more intentional plants, but its different leaf pattern had given it away. "Humans are masters of pattern recognition," my friend said. "But until a pattern is pointed out to them, they remain befuddled by what they see."

That was certainly the case with me and my garden. And it's often true of our work in organizations and communities. We don't really understand what we're looking at or why some things work and others don't. Once we understand the basic patterns, though, things become clearer. We are no longer befuddled. We see the patterns easily and everywhere. And we can act as more effective stewards of those systems. This is the value of pointing out a set of simple patterns common to all living systems, including organizations, economies and communities.

Although theories abound and there is little consensus about the definitive list of characteristics, following is the set of four properties I have found to be widely cited across the literature in biology and also universally present across the organizations and communities I have observed. Whether it is your body, a rainforest, an organization, or a community, these are the factors at play:

1. **Divergent Parts:** In every living system, there are individual parts – for example, the cells in our bodies and the people in an organization or community. This is "who I am" within the system.

   Generally, the more diverse and self-expressive the parts are able to be, the more resilient, adaptive and creative the living system is likely to be. This is the principle of biodiversity.

   In our human systems (e.g., organizations and communities), that means we have to create conditions that invite each person's unique expression and contribution – that enable them to bring as much of their particular strengths, talents and perspectives as possible – even as they are nourished in the process.

2. **A Pattern of Relationship:** The divergent parts are connected and supported in a pattern of responsive relationship with each other and with context.

   In our bodies, this is the interdependent systems that regulate circulation, digestion and temperature regulation, as well as the supportive skeletal structure. In organizations, it's the patterns and infrastructure of information-sharing, decision-making and getting things done: the org chart, processes, meetings, shared vocabulary, office design and equipment. In a community, we find it in the roads and traffic rules, retail infrastructure, governance systems and the culture of the commons. This is "how we are together" within and around the system.

   Generally, the more open and free-flowing the interactions between parts, the more resilient, adaptive and creative the living system is likely to be.

In our organizations, communities and families, this means we have to design structures and systems that support effective connection and collaboration with consistency but also with flexibility and responsiveness.

3. **A Convergent Whole:** The divergent parts come together in relationship to form a convergent whole with new characteristics and capabilities.

    This is the level not of your cells, but of you and your body. It is the level not of the individuals, but of the organization or community they create together. It is here that we find the phenomenon of emergence, in which new capabilities and characteristics are created, in the same way the properties of water (wetness, fluidity) emerge from the convergence of hydrogen and oxygen. This is the great promise of living systems – that new things become possible and new forms take shape. *You* can think, feel and move – capabilities not found at the level of your cells. Similarly, an organization or community is able to complete complex tasks and maintain order, even when those functions lie beyond the abilities of the people who comprise it.

    Just as the living system needs the seeming chaos of divergence, it also needs convergent order at the level of the whole. *You* remain recognizably *you*, even as your cells are continuously replaced. An organization remains focused on shared purpose, even as people come and go. A community retains its character across generations. This is "*who* we are together" and "*why* we are together" as a system.

    Generally, the more consistency and convergence there is at the level of the whole, the more resilient, adaptive and creative the living system is likely to be.

    Within our human groups, this means the shared purpose that brings us together must be both clear and compelling, and it must continuously guide our individual and collective actions.

4. **Self-Integration:** The entire process of divergence, relationship and convergence is self-organizing, set into motion by life itself.

    In the dynamic, moment-by-moment interplay of the first three properties, the living system is able to self-organize in order to innovate, adapt and ultimately generate higher, more complex forms of life (none of which can be done by a machine, by the way). Importantly, the process must be *self*-integrative – integrating parts into relationship and wholeness without an external engineer or manager. Even the single-celled amoeba involves too much complexity for us to orchestrate manually. And in effortlessly self-organizing, that amoeba demonstrates astonishing intelligence, creativity and even beauty.

    With the right fertile conditions in place – the right levels of divergence and convergence, and the right supportive structure and flow of interactions – our organizations and communities are poised similarly to astonish us with their self-organized wisdom, creativity and ease. This means that our most appropriate and important role is not to tightly control the activities of our human systems, but to cultivate the necessary fertile conditions for life to self-organize and self-integrate within them – creating space for people to sense what is needed, to respond wisely and effectively, and to learn and evolve both themselves and the system. Beyond management and leadership, this is stewarding life.

These are the "design principles" we have to work with in seeking to enable any living organization or community to thrive.

The following four chapters will explore how these patterns are present in multiple spheres of our lives, which together shape our perception and experience of the world. They reveal how – despite apparent evidence to the contrary – humanity is moving along a clear path in the direction of thriving, but that our arrival at that destination is far from guaranteed. And they provide evidence that conscious participation in these patterns offers the most promising way forward.

2.2

Science's Unfolding Explanation of Life

Though it may not be immediately evident, science's explanation of life directly influences the ways we perceive the world, the ways we make decisions, the ways we relate to each other, and the ways we live our lives. That explanation is currently in flux. With only slight delay, so are our perceptions, choices, relationships, and the most fundamental aspects of our lives.

The Machine Story

In the outgoing era, science explained the world as a controllable, predictable machine made up of inherently separate components. Perhaps most associated with this explanation is Sir Isaac Newton, who introduced the idea that the world could be understood by examining and controlling its smallest parts, each of which interacts only with its immediate neighbors in a linear progression. "Every action has an equal and opposite reaction," Newton assured us. And the entire world could be mapped and predicted according to a limited number of mathematical principles.

On the basis of this explanation, we came to understand ourselves, our communities and our organizations in this way. To a significant degree, it has guided and determined:

- The way we are born – into an impersonal hospital in a production-line procedure that is maximally efficient and cost-effective.
- The way we manage our health and illness – separating care into rigid specializations, overlooking the individual's role in health, and trusting only observable phenomena.
- The way we are educated – in a setting replicating factory life, with emphasis on rote memorization of data and socialization into an obedient system that is standardized and focused on individual output.
- The things we learn – practical, tangible skills and the natural laws of the physical world, typically, with only one right answer possible.
- Our entire food system – from single-crop agriculture and factory farms to the relentless drive for speed and convenience in our eating habits.
- The way we judge success and failure – according to external, material measures, like wealth and title.
- How we work – often in cubicles, according to segregated job descriptions, with supervisors judging our performance according to physical output.
- How we govern and are governed – in a system comprised of a small number of opposing parties, in which the statistical majority of people is assumed to have the right view and the minority the wrong view.
- How we die – in a maximally efficient and cost-effective nursing home, with our bodies submitted into a corpse-processing system.

These are the common choices and assumptions that made sense to us based on the perceptual filters of the past era.

Nowhere was the machine story more present than in business, where the company was considered a discrete, non-human entity that exists to make money by the most efficient means possible. Production and consumption were considered to be the sole purpose of all economic activity, with land, labor and capital as the means. Evolving value came to be achieved by increasing production efficiency – building bigger factories with diminishing variance in the production line, in order to achieve cheaper production costs per unit. Variance was the enemy. In a sentiment characteristic of the times, Henry Ford said famously of his Model

T, "You can paint it any color, so long as it's black." Frederick Taylor took things another step further, applying mechanistic theories to human endeavor with his *Principles of Scientific Management.* People were a factor of production to be employed, a cost to be reduced or eliminated. Inherently variable, they were seen as expendable, interchangeable, and, most of all, to be standardized as much as possible. Workers were organized into different departments with physical separation into tasks or cubicles. Tasks were further divided into standardized skills and competencies.

In all, it was as if the nature of life and our economic entities were viewed on one dimension:

The Mechanistic Model

Variance   Efficiency

But starting just over a hundred years ago, a growing series of insights forced us to reconsider our assumptions about how the world works. Science began to recognize that much of life evades linear, reductionist analysis, control and prediction. Key spheres of life – things as far-reaching as the weather, ecosystems, traffic patterns, the economy, bacteria, and ant colonies – each consistently fell outside the convenient constraints of Newton's laws.

What's more, in our organizations, we began to recognize that what we gained in mechanistic reduction and efficiency, we lost in integrity (meaning wholeness and interdependence). And what we lost in integrity, we also lost in creativity and flexibility. Consumers gradually gained the economic power to demand variety and quality, challenging the heavy, stagnant Mechanistic Model. Advancing technology shifted the nature of work to service, information and knowledge – necessarily variable contributions. And it became increasingly clear a linear model based on rising statistical efficiency of parts was no longer sufficient for sustained economic competitiveness.

As we found the reductionist cause-and-effect model insufficient, we turned again to science. And in reaction, science responded sheepishly, "Well, yes, it appears there is more to the story." Indeed, it owned up to a whole new chapter.

This new chapter began by distinguishing between "complication" and its counterpart, "complexity." Michael Lissack and Johan Roos have explained the distinction in their book, *The Next Common Sense*.

> In Latin, plic is "fold" and "plex" is weave." We fold to hide facets of things and to cram more into a crowded space – this is complicated. We weave to make use of connections and to introduce mutual dependencies – this is complex.[3]

In the book *More Space*, Johnnie Moore gives helpful examples of the two concepts:

> The wiring on an aircraft is complicated. To figure out where everything goes would take a long time. But if you studied it for long enough, you could know with (near) certainty what each electrical circuit does and how to control it. The system is ultimately knowable. If understanding it is important, the effort to study it and make a detailed diagram of it would be worthwhile.
>
> So complicated = not simple, but ultimately knowable.

> Now, put a crew and passengers in that aircraft and try to figure out what will happen on the flight. Suddenly we go from complicated to complex. You could study the lives of all these people for years, but you could never know all there is to know about how they will interact. You could make some guesses, but you can never know for sure. And the effort to study all the elements in more and more detail will never give you that certainty.
>
> So complex = not simple and never fully knowable. Just too many variables interact.[4]

With this distinction, we see that the outgoing worldview's attempt to understand entities by studying only their discrete parts was appropriate for complicated systems. Humankind has succeeded in controlling much of the physical world and in developing robust scientific knowledge by applying such an analytical method – by breaking a problem into components, studying each part in isolation, and then drawing conclusions about the whole. But for complex systems, with their variable patterns of relationships, a different explanation and approach are needed. And life, as it turns out, is decidedly complex.

Systems Thinking

Enter systems thinking, which introduces the simple yet profound notion that 'the whole is greater than the sum of its parts.' If reductionism focused on the *divergence* of parts, systems thinking was interested in their *interrelatedness*. As *Wall Street Journal* business writer Thomas Petzinger explains in his book *The New Pioneers*, "If Newtonianism sought understanding by taking things apart (the process called 'analysis'), systems thinking sought understanding things by putting them together ('synthesis')."[5]

The more science entertained this approach, the more it appeared that putting things together was the true nature of life. Howard Bloom explains this in a chapter called "Superorganism" in his book, *The Lucifer Principle*. According to Bloom, more than a hundred years ago German botanist Matthius Schleiden observed that the life and behavior of an organism comes from the way in which the individual cells work together. Pathologist Rudolph Virchow then added to this, declaring that "[t]he composition of the major organism, the so-called individual, must be likened to a kind of social arrangement or society, in which a number of separate existencies are dependent upon one another...." Each human being, said Virchow, is actually a society of separate cells.[6]

Indeed, the pattern of interaction extends beyond the organism to its environment, enabling a system to sense and adapt to ongoing changes in its habitat. In this view, Darwin's "survival of the fittest" becomes more fully understood as survival of the most continuously fit in ever-changing circumstances.

In fact, Darwin himself wrote a second, generally overlooked book, *Descent of Man*, in which he described relationship as the true driving force for evolution, particularly human evolution. In his book *Darwin's Unfolding Revolution*, David Loye reveals that Darwin showed "how cooperation and education as well as moral sensitivity and love were prime drivers not only of the evolution of our species, but in advancing incremental degrees over time, of all species."[7]

Relationship has another important effect. The web of interactions in a system enables a tiny change in initial conditions to alter the long-term behavior of the system drastically. This is the famous "Butterfly Effect," in which the mere flapping of a butterfly's wings in Latin America is presumed to be able to change the weather pattern in Florida. Whereas Newton assured us every action invariably has an equal and opposite reaction, now we see that in complex environments, small actions can trigger large, reverberating and decidedly *unequal* reactions.

Even more fascinating than such an unpredictable chain reaction of responses is the related phenomenon of emergence. As *divergent parts* interact in *relationship* to create a new, *convergent whole*, all complex systems exhibit emergent behaviors. As Harvard University pathology professor Donald Ingber explains:

An organism, whether it is a bacterium or a baboon, develops through an incredibly complex series of interactions involving a vast number of different components. These components, or subsystems, are themselves made up of smaller molecular components, which independently exhibit their own dynamic behavior, such as the ability to catalyze chemical reactions. Yet when they are combined into some larger functioning unit – such as a cell or tissue – utterly new and unpredictable properties emerge, including the ability to move, to change shape and to grow.[8]

Systems that at first glance seem vastly different – ant colonies, human brains, cities, and immune systems – all demonstrate the property of emergence. And author and biologist Michael Colebrook notes that this tendency exists at every level of life.

> Forests exhibit emergent properties based on relationships between living organisms. Living organisms show emergent properties based on relationships between complex chemicals. Complex chemicals show emergent properties based on the relationships between atoms. Atoms show emergent properties based on the relationships between sub-atomic particles.... Given the ubiquity of emergent processes and the way in which they are organised into progressive sequences, it can be argued that they are the means by which the universe creates itself.[9]

In this way, we see that in every complex system, agents residing on one scale start producing behavior that lies a scale above them. Such emergent characteristics only occur if parts are working together; they do not occur from the operation of any single part alone. Thus, understanding each part as it operates independently does not offer insight into the nature of the whole – just as understanding hydrogen and oxygen does not offer insight into the nature of water. And with this, we see that the evolution of life is derived not only from chance modifications, but also from innovative combinations and interactions. Just as Darwin observed random genetic mutations as fundamental to the evolution of life, science has recognized complex patterns of relationship as intrinsic to the origin, development and survival of any living system.

With this insight, systems thinking effectively challenged five hundred years of reductionist, mechanistic paradigm.

In time, this evolving understanding of life gradually began to shape business. The company was revealed as a convergent whole, with emergent characteristics of its own, distinct from those of the individuals comprising it. And the web of relationships was acknowledged to be the primary contributing factor to this emergence.

As early as the 1950s, W. Edwards Deming proposed that "the performance of anyone is governed largely by the system that he works in."[10] Though initially rejected by US companies, his ideas were readily accepted by their Japanese counterparts, whose subsequent market dominance in many industries served as the first systems thinking wake-up call to American industry.

In more recent years, systems proponent Peter Senge pointed out that "Business and other human endeavors are...bound by invisible fabrics of interrelated actions, which often take years to fully play out their effects on each other."[11] To understand a problem fully, he advised, it is necessary to look also at feedback loops – the self-reinforcing pattern of relationships within a system. In a simple example, "a worker gets caught working overtime so much that relationships at home deteriorate and it gets more and more 'painful' to go home, which, of course, makes the worker even more likely to neglect home life in the future."[12]

Industry has made notable strides in integrating systems theory within still-dominant mechanistic practices. Team-building hit an unprecedented high in the past few decades in an effort to nurture the valuable web of relationships within a company. Customer Relationship Management and market research were honed into a sharp science as companies sought greater responsiveness to their environment. And efforts were taken to create dynamic corporate cultures, with the hope of creating wholes greater than the sum of their parts.

In these ways, attention expanded beyond the individual parts to include the relationships connecting them, as well as the convergent whole that resulted from those interactions, with its new, emergent characteristics. Within this perspective, it was as if life, including our economic entities, could now be seen in two dimensions, as illustrated in the following diagram

The Systems Model

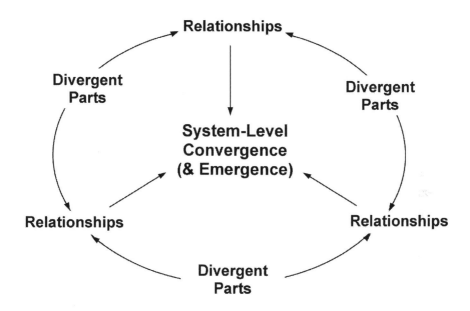

And while all of this represented an important shift in emphasis, it did not usher in a truly meaningful revision to our guiding ideology. Instead, systems thinking remained (and still generally remains) grounded in a mechanistic model, simply making more of the machine visible.

Consider as evidence this definition by systems theorist Alan Scrivener:

Systems theory is the study of systems which can be mapped using any kind of network to define the flow of information. This includes the study of systems whose emergent properties we cannot yet predict due to a lack of plausible mechanisms, rigorous mapping techniques and/or robust mathematical treatment.[13]

Or consider the 2006 book by Eric Beinhocker, *The Origin of Wealth*, which recognizes the economy as an emergent property...but then applies computer modeling to try to predict economic outcomes.[14]

Or note this assertion by Chilean biologists Humberto Maturana and Francisco Varela: "We maintain that living systems are machines... and hence, that [they] can be explained ... in terms of relations, not of component properties."[15]

As if simply another set of gears had been added, the prevailing view seems to be that a system can still be predicted – and perhaps controlled – with more advanced (albeit yet-to-be-discovered) equations and methods. The common assumption seems to be that the landscape remains fundamentally the same but with added details. With this understanding, systems thinking expands our view beyond the individual parts to higher-level patterns of behavior between multiple parts. And while this is a valuable advancement in thought, according to this perspective, a mechanistic paradigm is still appropriate. The mechanism has simply gotten more complex.

As a result, the systems model was widely interpreted in business as a call for overarching structure as a means of efficiently achieving organizational goals. This view emphasized the role of management in deciding such structures and in determining the specific goals to be achieved. The result was heavy focus on rigid specificity of goals and formalization of rules and roles. Reorganization and re-engineering became the strategy of choice. The continuing metaphor of the machine was ever present.[16]

Even Deming's forward-looking systems vision was implemented in mechanistic fashion. Though he insisted that measurement and quotas be replaced with leadership and removal of fear from the workplace, the widespread application of his concepts has focused squarely on statistical measurement. As one Deming devotee testified: "Reducing variation, or continual improvement, is the great promise of Deming's methods."[17]

Of course, this is a generalization. There are enlightened souls in any industry who stretch beyond these incomplete simplifications. But for the most part, research reveals the persistence of mechanistic thinking that is valuable to some degree and absurd if taken as the total view. The result is that many of the changes made to date on the basis of systems thinking represent important first steps in a new direction, while most have been superficial and built on familiar values. In summary, the Systems Model has been a limited and temporary bridge.

As life continued to evade control and prediction – despite an expanded model – science again was pressed for further explanation. And again it responded with hesitant acknowledgment of yet another chapter to the story.

LIVING SYSTEMS THINKING

Revealed only a few decades ago, the plot of this next chapter in science's story revolves around the property that some biologists call "self-integration." This property is the main characteristic that distinguishes *me* from *my car*. After all, both my car and I contain diverse parts – engine, brakes, steering wheel, in the case of my car; cells and organs in the case of my body. Both function through interactions between parts and with the outside world. In both cases, divergent parts and a dynamic pattern of interactions come together to form a convergent whole with new characteristics not present at the level of the parts – the parts of my car come together to form a vehicle that has the new capability to move me around town; my cells and organs come together to make me a thinking, feeling, moving human being. Previously, this is where the comparison ended. And with such clear similarities, I was believed – literally – to be a machine, just like my car. "Living systems are chemical automata," says one author in a book called, ironically, *The Nature of Life*. "We shall consider living systems as fluid machines," says another.[18]

But in recent years, biologists have begun to recognize a key differentiating factor. Without this factor, my car can't generate itself – or a new car. It will never have a great idea. It will never repair itself. It is not resilient, adaptive or creative. But I am.

What distinguishes me from my car, science now tells us, is the property or capability of **"self-integration."**[19] This means that – **by itself** – every living system **integrates** divergent parts into a convergent whole characterized by dynamic relationship internally and externally in a continuous process of **self-organization** and **self-creation**.

This concept can best be illustrated with a simple example: the sea sponge. Though they look like plants, sea sponges are actually multi-cellular animals. What is most interesting about them is that if you push a sea sponge through a super-fine sieve, breaking free its individual cells, those cells will move about and act as independent, single-celled amoeba. But after some time, they will find each other, form connections, and recreate themselves as a single whole sponge. In other words, they will self-integrate.[20] And with this re-integrated whole, we find emergent characteristics that were not present for the independent cells: we find pores and tunnels, new reproductive patterns, the ability to digest relatively large prey, and the capacity to house other creatures.

This is a striking example of the underlying tendency and urge of all life to connect with other life to generate emergent, transcendent forms. It is what Lebanese poet Kahlil Gibran calls "life's longing for itself." And it is what drives us to create families and organizations and communities.

This phenomenon is also sometimes called autopoiesis, which means "self-creation." In his paper on the topic, complexity scientist Chris Lucas explains:

This biologically based theory...defines life as the ability to self-produce, rather than as (conventionally) the ability to reproduce.... This definition of life is far better than the systemic illogicality of defining it as the reproduction of a passive gene. A living system is an ongoing process that self-defines and self-maintains its form; reproduction is not a necessary function of this.[21]

Physicist Per Bak refers to this as the "self-organised criticality" – self-organized because no engineer had a hand in it, critical because it balances moment by moment at a critical point between order and chaos – between convergence and divergence.[22]

According to physicist Fritjof Capra, the inherent tendency to self-organize is not a product of blind genetic trial-and-error, as Darwin originally asserted, nor of linear cause-and-effect as Newton would have us believe. Instead it is "an unfolding of order and divergence analogous to a learning process, including both independence from the environment and freedom of choice."[23] As a system approaches a critical point, "it 'decides' which way to go, and this decision determines its evolution."[24] Biologist Lyall Watson asserts similarly that evolution is guided by chance, but that chance has "a pattern and a reason of its own."[25] And zoologist Jacob von Uexkull claims that "The organism is not merely a reactor to the environment, but an operator upon its...scene."[26]

Evolutionary biologist Stuart Kauffman concurs:

Whether we are talking about molecules cooperating to form cells or organisms cooperating to form ecosystems or buyers and sellers cooperating to form markets and economies, we will find grounds to believe that Darwinism is not enough, that natural selection cannot be the sole source of the order we see in the world. In crafting the living world, selection has always acted on systems that exhibit spontaneous order.[27]

On the basis of this new understanding, new theories of the evolution of life emerged. Darwin focused on chance divergence – nature makes mistakes along the way and sometimes those mistakes prove to be advantageous. They are, then, naturally selected and become the norm. Now, in addition (some would say instead), science observes that: (1) the living system exhibits a self-regulating "intelligence" that actively integrates successful mutations into an orderly whole, all the while maintaining a critical and dynamic balance between chaos and order; and (2) the system sometimes autonomously generates divergence and novel combinations, seemingly in order to maintain critical balance and to strengthen itself. And so, the other side of the Darwinian coin seems to be self-regulation and self-transcendence (meaning, the ability to combine to create higher level, transcendent forms of life).[28]

In fact, it may be that there are *not* two different sides to this coin at all. Even Darwin's random mutation theory can be explained in the context of this self-organized quest for transcendence. Ilya Prigogine and his colleagues won the Nobel Prize for showing that under appropriate conditions chemical systems pass through randomness before evolving into higher levels of self-organized structures. This finding has been used as the basis for integrating Darwinian natural selection into complexity science, with the conclusion that it is the self-organizing property that generates random mutations as a means of facilitating evolution to a higher level of species. **Those mutations are not mistakes; they're innovations.**

The nature of complex living systems is thus revealed as intrinsically dynamic and integrative. And the natural world is found to be inherently adaptive and creative. Not only that, its creativity is self-generated. A look at the etymology of the word "integrate" reveals just how appropriate it is for our new understanding: it comes from 'intus-gerere,' which means 'to generate inside.'

Thus, we now understand that a living system consists of **interwoven relationships** between **distinct, locally acting parts** that together make up **a coherent whole.** Those relationships include responsiveness to changes from context and from within the system itself. And this generative - and regenerative - process is set in motion and sustained by a **self-regulating and self-integrating property**.

With this insight, science's expanded story offers us the basic prescription for a living system to thrive, whether it is a rainforest, an ant colony, an organization, or you and your body. For a living system to be fully resilient, adaptive and creative, the following fertile conditions must be present:

1. **Divergent Parts:** We know from the concept of biodiversity that a thriving living system must have sufficient levels of divergence. If it is to be resilient, it can't put all its eggs in one basket. And if it is to be adaptable and creative, it must be able to create novel combinations.

    But if the system has only divergence (or too much of it), it remains a shapeless crowd of individuals, with no apparent boundary. This is total chaos, or entropy, and this state renders the system incapable of concerted effort.

2. **A Pattern of Relationships:** In a thriving living system, the divergent parts are connected in a dynamic pattern and network of relationships, including the infrastructure to support those relationships. In other words, the means exist for internal and external feedback. In our bodies, this is the circulatory system, the digestive and immune systems, the supporting skeletal system. In organizations, this is the patterns and infrastructure of information-sharing, decision-making and getting work done.

   Again, there is an appropriate level of interaction and information flow. Too little and the system will become stagnant; too much and it will be chaotic.[29]

3. **A Convergent Whole:** A living system also needs sufficient levels of convergence, or order. Your body maintains homeostasis. *You* remain recognizably *you* even as your cells are continuously replaced. An organization remains focused on a clear, shared purpose even as people come and go. There is a clear, convergent identity that remains relatively consistent over time at the level of the whole. On this basis, the living system is able to generate the phenomenon of emergence, in which new capabilities are created.

   And yet, too much convergence leads to rigidity and homogeneity. This renders the system incapable of change – a deadly situation. Again, just the right mix of divergence and convergence is needed, with continuous adjustments according to changing circumstances.

4. **Self-Integration:** In a dynamic interplay of the first three conditions, the living system is able to self-organize in order to innovate, adjust and ultimately, create higher, more complex forms of life.

   And here's the thing: it must be <u>self</u>-integrative. As we noted in the opening chapter of this section: even an amoeba is far too complex for us to manage and control. Yet in its effortless capacity to self-organize, the amoeba shows an amazing capability to thrive. So, too, with our organizations and communities, when the right conditions are established.

This four-part pattern is present at every level of life – including our organizations, economies and communities, which are revealed as a higher level of life created by the interactions of the people and institutions within them. Indeed, many scientists believe the Earth itself is a single, living, self-regulating entity. Known as the Gaia Hypothesis, the theory holds that (as Vaclav Havel explained it in a powerful speech called *The Need for Transcendence*), "the dense network of mutual interactions between the organic and inorganic portions of the earth's surface form a single system, a kind of mega-organism, a living planet."[30]

With this broader understanding, life can now be viewed not as a one-dimensional spectrum or a two-dimensional feedback loop, but as a three-dimensional process, actively creating from its environment. The following diagram portrays one metaphor for how we might envision this process: as a three-sided prism or pyramid.

The Living Systems Model

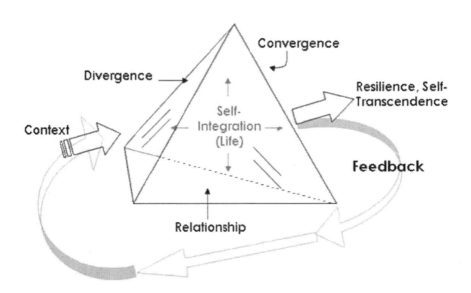

Within this metaphor, context from the environment enters the system as a source of energy, a change in surroundings, a new idea.

In reaction, the living system integrates divergent responses (the first face of the pyramid), sparking a flurry of relationships (the second face) and shaping or reshaping the convergent whole (the third face). Most importantly, the integrative property fills the center of our conceptual prism, setting the whole process in motion.

According to this metaphor, if any of the three facets of the prism are not fully "polished" – if they're not present at optimal levels and coherent with each other – then the internal self-regulating property will not be able to shine through and do its self-integrative "thing." And the living system will not thrive, at least not to its full potential. It's as if all three faces must be clear and free of tarnish in order for the core self-integrating property to generate full thrivability.

What is generated, then, is emergent or transcendent patterns of behavior – a higher level in life's hierarchy, like a sea sponge, or your body, or an organization. Along the way, the living system learns through feedback. And the whole living process is creative, adaptive and regenerative by its nature.

Living Organizations

Understanding these patterns has important implications for us in our lives, our work and our world. In organizations – or in any collective human endeavor – it helps us see that:

- We have to nurture optimal levels of **divergence**, enabling individuals to bring the best of themselves – their talents, their unique perspectives and insights, their ability to identify opportunities and to contribute solutions, their drive for meaning, their authenticity, their quirks, their passion. The more of these that are invited, the more life and vitality people will bring into the organization.

- We must also cultivate useful and dynamic **patterns of relationship**, creating appropriately supportive and guiding structures, processes, information flow and trust. In fact, this is normally what we think of as "the organization" – its assets, its policies and processes, its culture.

- We also have to serve the customer or community compellingly. This is the shared purpose that brings us together in any organization. And shared purpose is what creates **convergence**, channeling individual divergence in clear service of a common cause and uniting people in wholeness and mutual identity. It is what elevates them beyond a shapeless crowd and enables concerted life-sustaining effort and the emergence of new characteristics and capabilities.

- Most important of all, the living systems patterns show us that our role as leaders is to create the conditions for the organization-as-living-ecosystem to **self-integrate** – to self-organize and to enable collective intelligence, responsiveness and resilience to emerge. This sometimes requires us to leave ample space and time for the unforeseen to rise to the surface, and at other times it calls for single-minded resolve and firm decisions. In this way, it makes us less like engineers (as in the Mechanistic Model), less like network modelers (as in the Systems Model) and more like gardeners or stewards.

None of this is new. These four elements have invariably been the factors that enabled organizations to thrive, even if we didn't always recognize them as such. Now, the living systems patterns help us understand how – and why the most pioneering, cutting edge practices are so effective. They also help us understand how those practices all fit together, so that it no longer makes sense to isolate brand strategy from internal culture, corporate strategy from office design, meeting design from human passions.

It is important to note that the Living Systems Model transcends and yet also includes the long-prevailing Mechanistic Model, acknowledging that there is still value in efficiency; there is simply more to the story. With the Systems Model, another dimension was acknowledged: the presence of rich interactions, system-level characteristics and feedback. But only with the Living Systems Model does our explanation of life take on full, dynamic creativity and intelligence.

The irony is that this latest model represents maximum efficiency (the original goal of the Mechanistic model) as we recognize the ability – and the *inclination* – of living systems to develop such high sensitivity that only a small change in context is needed to create a specialized response. We see this in today's most vibrant organizations, as companies like Google react adeptly to changes in the market and companies like Apple introduce innovations that we never imagined, but suddenly can't live without.

THE SPARK OF LIFE

The big question that remains, then, is: what exactly is this all-important integrative property at the center of the Living Systems Model? Without this core attribute, even the most tightly interwoven system is no more animated than a telephone network connecting a group of people who have nothing to say to each other. The connections alone will not achieve self-creation and regeneration; *something more* must be present to galvanize the network – something that sparks integration and moves the system toward self-transcendence.

Fundamentally, this "something more" is *life*, isn't it? It's whatever animates us and makes us alive. It's the basic difference between me and my car.

Going further, we might describe it as "the animating or vital principle in man (and animals); that which gives life to the physical organism, in contrast to its purely material elements; the breath of life."

The quote above is the *Oxford English Dictionary*'s definition of "spirit."

And yet the word spirit typically comes with heavy religious baggage, which is unfortunate since it seems to be the most accurate and complete term, implying non-physicality, integrality (referring to the underlying wholeness and interconnectedness of the world) and animation. Any substitute seems to be an incomplete euphemism that (1) fails to convey the full sense of integrality, (2) leaves us comfortably within a mechanistic paradigm, or (3) strips the concept of its wonder – which one could argue is an important missing element in today's dominant guiding story. In rejecting the term out of hand, we may be throwing the baby out with the bathwater when we close the door on an informed, wonder-filled recognition of the intangible, unifying essence of life at the same time that we reject limiting religious practices and beliefs.

Instead, I wonder if we might move toward a new definition of "spirit" as "a universal quality of connection, purpose, integration and awareness that transcends religions and exists apart from religions as well."[31] Such a definition would allow us to integrate science and spirituality – not the religious dogma that so often seeks to control and divide, but the basic message common to the world's wisdom traditions (the Perennial Philosophy, as Aldous Huxley called it) that life is integral, self-organizing and creative by its nature. Einstein declared: "I believe in Spinoza's God who reveals himself in the orderly harmony of what exists." To 17th century philosopher Baruch Spinoza, God and nature were one, "the deterministic system of which everything in nature is a part." Today's science seems to be moving toward increasing agreement with Spinoza, offering us a chance to reconcile our objective observations about reality with centuries of subjective beliefs.

In the end, it doesn't really matter what you call this non-physical, unifying, animating and integrative realm. Call it a self-integrating property, as some biologists do. Call it life, as I do, or even the spark or essence of life. Call it the unified field, or the "zero point field," as many scientists do. Ancient Chinese healers recognized it as Chi. Indian Ayurvedic practitioners call it Prana. Management experts Peter Senge and Otto Scharmer call it Source. My husband and George Lucas call it The Force. Creativity expert Julia Cameron suggests "Good Orderly Direction."

Whatever term you choose, the evidence is overwhelming that life depends on the active presence of this underlying source of order and creativity. Abundantly available, set into place and into action effortlessly and inexplicably in nature, in ourselves and in our communities, this source of "aliveness" must first be present *and* its integrative spark must burn brightly in order for a complex system to connect, create, regenerate and, ultimately, transcend itself. And as the world becomes more complex, your success in life and work will increasingly depend on your ability to engage this core property.

THE COLLECTIVE NATURE OF LIFE

Indeed, not only must we acknowledge the active presence of this integrative realm of life, we must also recognize its group-level dynamics. Scientists have yet to discover what compels cells to divide and choose complementary roles, or by what means bees discern which role they should fill, or – for that matter – what drives people to come together within an organization or a community. But the latest findings would suggest that this underlying essence of life runs through each part and also through the whole, connecting all, as an unbroken thread. It is this common thread that enables the coordinated activities of the whole and that creates not just interconnectedness but *integrality*, in which parts are clearly distinct and divergent but also not truly separate from the whole or from each other. In other words, the essence of life that animates you cannot be considered separate from the life that animates your cells or your organs, nor can it be considered separate from the trees whose air you breathe, from the animals whose flesh you eat, or indeed from any other living thing on Earth.

As we note the ordered integrality of all life, we're able to recognize that the life that flows within and unites all of us has a clear propensity, which is the pursuit of ever higher levels of emergence and self-transcendence. And with such an understanding, we can see that this is in no way disenfranchising, as past religious claims of a guiding "higher power" have often seemed. Instead it seems more appropriate to speak of an inner and at the same time all-encompassing essence or property. It seems more accurate to speak of our active and increasingly conscious *participation* in a "wise" living system that may well be learning along the way, as it seeks to connect to itself in novel ways. And each of us represents an infinite source of novelty.

Given this understanding, we see again that the goal of life is most likely *not* steady input and output, punctuated by occasional mutations and disruptions, as the mechanistic worldview would have us believe. Humans do not exist and function simply to pass on genes. That process would likely have been too slow for life's taste. In fact, we evolve culturally much faster than we do genetically, bringing us into daily awareness of the patterns and larger goal of all life: to connect to itself in ever more complex forms through an endless learning cycle of divergence, relationship, convergence and, most importantly, integration.

With this observation, science has firmly erected the first signpost pointing toward a new paradigm – a new "way of knowing." Its expanded account has helped to usher in a worldview in which all life is recognized as a single interwoven tapestry of living, evolving, creative organisms. And at the core of this new worldview is a deeper understanding of the patterns and proclivities of the animating, integrative spark of life.

Again, it may seem that these findings have little relevance to our daily lives. But science discovers only what the evolving perceptual framework lets into view. Therefore, this signpost is ultimately an indication of profound changes taking place in society at large. These changes open the door to a fundamental revision of our every strategy, choice and expectation. As we come to understand more about the possibilities inherent in engaging the life in our organizations and communities, it's like discovering a superpower we never knew we had – the power to unleash unprecedented wisdom, collaboration, creativity and impact.

Aspects of Living Systems

Aspect	Description
Parts	• Distinct, diverse, dynamic. • Exert pressure toward chaos and divergence. • Parts exist, evolve and are defined in relationship to the whole, to other parts in the system, and to context. • Every part is itself a whole living system, down to the sub-atomic level.
Relationship	• The network, infrastructure and pattern of communication and interaction between parts, whole and context. • Reflects the responsive and evolving nature of living systems, equivalent to learning. As the system evolves in reaction to changes in its context, it becomes increasingly integrated with its environment. In this way, it becomes increasingly sensitive to changes in the context, driving more evolution, in turn driving infinite and unpredictable creativity.
Whole	• Collective, convergent. • Exerts pressure toward order and coherence. • The whole takes on properties of its own that cannot be understood by examining the parts. • Every whole system is a part of a higher-order system, out to the far reaches of the cosmos.

Integration	<ul><li>Enabled by the essence, spirit or spark of life.</li><li>The self-organizing property of continuously enfolding divergent parts within a convergent whole.<ul><li>Excess convergence creates stagnation, death.</li><li>Excess divergence creates chaos, death.</li><li>Dynamic balance between the two creates coherence, evolution and the conditions for "aliveness" and thriving.</li></ul></li><li>Creates a whole greater than the sum of its parts.</li><li>Must increase with rising complexity.</li><li>The integrative property is observed to generate system divergence of its own accord (if necessary) to support a dynamic balance and, presumably to support further evolution.</li></ul>
Context	<ul><li>The environment (energy, matter, information) of which the system is an integral part.</li><li>Continually acts on the system of whole and parts, introducing novelty and opportunity.</li><li>The whole exists as part of, is defined by, and evolves within its context.</li></ul>
Transcendence	<ul><li>The natural and continuous urge and outcome of the living combination of divergent parts, convergent whole, relationship, integration and context – a higher level, more complex form of life is created.</li><li>Reflects the living system's emergent capability to generate new forms, as well as to regenerate, evolve, react, adapt and innovate.</li><li>Represents the fundamental creative nature of complex adaptive living systems.</li></ul>

2.3

The Evolution of our Social Context

I̶N ADDITION TO science's explanation of reality, our "way of knowing" is also a function of the social context in which we live – the content, nature and tone of our interactions with others, as well as our beliefs about those interactions. While views about social context vary from person to person, there are clearly dominant trends within any culture and within each major era. And so any examination of worldviews – including one with thriving and thrivability at its core – must also explore social context.

With such an exploration, we find that our human communities exhibit the trademark features of living systems: the increasingly *divergent* contributions of individuals united in dynamic *relationship* within *convergent* communities of all forms and sizes, generating ever greater forms of *transcendence* (e.g., families, tribes, nations, companies, sports teams, communities, as well as their novel outputs).

A New Lens on Humanity's Four Major Eras

As we might expect, social context evolves over time. What is surprising, though, is that in its evolution, humanity seems to have concentrated on honing each of the four major attributes of living systems *in succession*. The following pages will take us on a brief historical tour, showing how our perceptions and interactions were convergent during the Hunter-Gatherer era; we focused on developing the capability of relation-ship during the Agrarian era; the Industrial Era and the centuries just preceding it were humanity's call to diverge *en masse*; and the early indications are that the emerging era will find humanity honing the skill of integration.

As we try to understand the major eras of human civilization, it is expedient and convenient to define them by their tools and practical methods of survival. The Age of the Spear advanced into the Era of the Plow, which grew into the Age of the Machine, which now blends into the Internet Era. Tribal villages evolved into farms, which gave way to factories, which eventually became office buildings and then home offices. According to this defining view, the key to successful evolution is as simple as keeping up with the latest technological advancements and real estate strategies. And, according to this definition, the transition between eras ought to be relatively speedy, with a new tool pushing out old habits within a few years of its acceptance.

But a more thorough and useful definition revolves around the critical ques-tion of *why* those distinctive tools and methods of survival were chosen at each stage. Each era of human civilization has had specific patterns of thought, par-ticular ways in which meanings and truths were constructed, and a fundamentally different consciousness of the world. At each stage, there has been a collective and distinguishing way of knowing. Within this defining view of the ages, then, each era's tools and methods have merely been artifacts characteristic of that period's dominant lens.

This isn't to say the earliest humans were incapable of relationship, divergence or integration; these were simply not the primary focus of those societies. And likewise, the focus of past eras hasn't disappeared as new ones entered the scene; those capa-bilities merely became less dominant. With each past transition *and* with this one, there is lengthy and at times turbulent overlap. The lens of the outgoing era remains in place but gradually loses its dominance. In other words, it never disappears but remains in the background as part of a fuller perceptual repertoire. Indeed, all facets must be present to some extent if life is to sustain itself. But historically, the "center of gravity" of any civilization has clearly focused on one aspect or another, as the following pages will demonstrate.

It is important not to interpret these different focal points as a basis for value judgment. Convergent consciousness is not naïve and wrong, as many modern observers have assumed; instead it represents a capability that continues to be critical for our survival. And divergent thought cannot be considered more evolved, intelligent or important than relationship consciousness. In fact, it is becoming ever clearer that the divergent lens is catastrophic if taken as the only reasonable perspective. **Each of the lenses is equally valid, representing a vital source of intelligence and capability. Together, they are the multiple faces of wisdom.**

And yet, the mind boggles at the idea of such a neat, orderly progression. Why on Earth should we believe that humanity evolves socially according to such a relatively linear path?

First, the path has not been precisely linear. Rather than interpreting the eras of humanity as a series of definitive shifts taken by all humans in lockstep, it may be more accurate to view each era as the appearance of a new option on the scene. At each transition, some parts of the human population began to experiment with an alternative focus, while others continued to steward one of the other core capabilities.

At any one point in history, then, different populations have held different focal points, though they may be contemporaries and even neighbors. Indeed, such variations explain much of global conflict today. For example, U.S. friction with Communist powers and the Middle East can be better understood as a clash between worldviews: the convergent Communist and Islamic nations must by their nature rub the strongly divergent United States the wrong way (and vice versa). Also, there have been many examples of civilizations that have returned to previous focal points (in Europe, for example, the Middle Ages were a return to relationship consciousness after the divergent and perhaps even integrative worldview of the Greek and Roman Empires).

If different societies today demonstrate different focal points, this may be cause not for derision or conflict, but for celebration: together, humanity has all the ingredients needed to reach full thrivability.

But this still leaves us wondering why such a relatively delineated path of social evolution has played out over human history.

Einstein famously remarked that there are two ways to look at life: one, as though nothing is a miracle; the other, as though everything is a miracle. The answer to our question about humanity's progression seems to fall into one (or a combination) of those two categories.

First, as though nothing is a miracle. Like any living system, humanity has always been challenged to increase its adaptability in the face of growing population and the resultant rise in complexity. As a group of people increases in number, it expands and comes into contact with new stimuli. As a result, the population must constantly increase its level of adaptability in order to survive these new encounters, which invariably introduce challenges to the status quo. In these ways, small nomadic tribes were challenged by increasing encounters with other tribes; early farmers were challenged by changing conditions; and office workers today are challenged by globalization. Humanity has responded to this mounting complexity by successively developing our capabilities to converge, relate, diverge and integrate. Within this view, these four capabilities are merely an expanded version of Darwin's "survival of the fittest." And we are merely reactive survivors.

Second, as though everything is a miracle. There are a growing number of scientists and philosophers who attribute an "evolutionary urge" to life. For them, life's propensity is to create ever greater forms of emergent transcendence. And the evolution of humanity is another point of evidence for this view. Not satisfied with the pace and output of genetic evolution, life initiated another method: cultural evolution, in which the generative pattern of life is played out in our interactions with each other and the world around us. On a geological scale, the result has been an astonishingly rapid development of the ingredients for thrivability. With this perspective, we have the opportunity to be active participants in a grand creative adventure.

I invite you to choose whichever perspective you like and bring it along as we embark on a rapid journey through human social evolution. There are many critical lessons for our times along the way.

The Era of Convergence

In the Hunter-Gatherer Era, convergence was the name of the game. The social context was experienced as an undivided wholeness, with hunter-gatherers understanding themselves as completely enmeshed in the surrounding world, perceiving no hard boundaries between self and other and existing only in present moment awareness and responsiveness.[32] On the basis of this relationship with the world, Erich Neumann notes in *The Origins and History of Consciousness* that Cro-Magnon humans "mov[ed] through the repetition and routine of a simple, nomadic life, with no distinct sense of self." This convergent social context remains evident even among modern-day hunter-gatherers. In a simple example, the greeting of a modern-day, isolated, cave-dwelling tribe in Mexico is "We are all one,"[33] and ethnic Mayans welcome each other with "Inlakesh" or "I am another yourself."

Some historians and anthropologists call this way of perceiving the world "animism," which one glossary defines as "the belief that all of nature is endowed with a pure life essence which holds all things in a symbiotic relationship and a spiritual balance within the universe."[34] As a result of this worldview, the vast majority of hunter-gatherer cultures include practices to tap into collective consciousness. Native American writer Gayle Highpine notes that:

Nearly all animistic cultures are also shamanistic cultures. That is to say, most animistic peoples live in a world that is not only alive and conscious, but also in which all consciousness is connected in a continuous field of living intelligence, rather than being locked inside individual brains as in mechanistic culture; a world in which spirits communicate guidance in dreams, in which telepathic closeness does not depend on physical closeness, and in which all our feelings and energies interflow and affect one another.[35]

Author Jean-François Noubel calls hunter-gatherers "the original collective intelligence."

When we examine these cultures through the modern (divergent) lens, we assume they were fearful, competing brutes. But in fact, this convergent worldview seems to have brought great happiness and a strong sense of belonging to members of hunter-gatherer tribes. Notes evolutionary psychiatrist Bruce Charlton:

The idea that people in simple hunter gatherer societies are 'happier' than either agricultural peasants or modern industrial-mercantile citizens ... has been amply confirmed.... This greater 'happiness' of hunter gatherers is twofold. A greater frequency and/or intensity of gratifying emotions on the one hand, and the integrated sense of feeling at home in the world on the other.[36]

Though these convergent perspectives are generally dismissed as naive or superstitious, in fact, the hunter-gatherer belief system has much to teach us today.

Indeed, the evidence indicates that we are all – in some important ways - still hunter-gatherers.

Dr. Michael Winkelman notes in *Shamanism and Cognitive Evolution*: "The universality of shamanic practices reflects underlying biologically structured foundations or *modes* of consciousness."[37] In other words, there's something about the way human beings are physically wired that made our ancestors pass through a phase of convergent consciousness, no matter where they lived.

And there is reason to believe that every child born today passes through such a phase, in which the context is perceived as a unified, convergent whole and the infant child experiences only the present moment.

This means that we all *had* a convergent perspective at one early time in our lives. As we move on to focus on relationship and then divergence, we generally dismiss these early convergent perspectives. But do we leave them behind? Perhaps not. There is increasing evidence that we just learn to ignore them and generally fail to develop them. But it seems that they remain part of the standard operating system of all humans.

For example, human development expert Joseph Chilton Pearce refers to the ability to access this collective consciousness as "the primary process," which he describes as: "the function through which we are conscious of the Earth as a thinking globe, the flow of life, the general field of awareness...." He notes: "Other cultures have maintained a much greater openness to the primary process than Western culture has...."[38]

Famed psychologist Carl Jung credited this type or level of awareness for the universal dream archetypes found in every culture, as well as for our experiences of meaningful and highly unlikely coincidence, which he called synchronicity. He believed that this collective level of consciousness is also a major source of our instincts and intuition. To him and others, it is this type of awareness we tap into in profound meditative states and flashes of inspiration.

And in recent decades, scientific evidence has been mounting in favor of such a shared (or at least connective) realm of awareness through experiments in group meditation, remote viewing, random number generation, and remote and shamanistic healing/prayer.

So, what if there really *is* a collective experience of the world? What if the hunter-gatherer stage of development *isn't* just childish, naive … and wrong? Instead, what if those of us in non-indigenous cultures have just denied and overlooked this world-view, to our detriment? And what if we could develop practices to tap into this aspect of ourselves intentionally?

It bears consideration.

As we will see in later chapters, there is reason to believe that actively reintegrating this convergent perspective may provide a powerful key to discovering greater meaning and happiness in life. It may *also* offer an important key to organizational success, as people learn to sense what is needed at the level of the whole organization and even the whole community. Indeed, it may very well be necessary for the sustainability of our species, as we re-learn how to sense and care for all life.

The Era of Relationship

As with all living systems, a rich form of relationship and connection was needed to foster greater adaptive and emergent capabilities among early humans. Such relationship, it seems, was the focus of the next era of development, as a new perceptual framework emerged and people became aware of the cyclical nature of the world and the connections between themselves and their environment.

Between 8,000 and 10,000 years ago, the development of agriculture offered the first major evidence of a heightened sense of self in relation to other. You cannot know that you are you - and distinctly, divergently so - until you are aware of and in relationship with other-than-you. Just as a young child develops a sense of self first in relation to surrounding objects and family members, the people of this next era gradually developed a sense of self, not in the full sense that we know it, but simply in relationship with other people and things. Thus, people became aware that they could *affect* nature by weeding wheat fields to improve their yield, by building fences around crops to keep animals out, by deliberately retaining and planting seeds. In this way, agriculture emerged within a relatively short period of time in four unrelated regions: the Middle East, the Far East, Central America, and the Andean region of South America.

Within the same time frame, humanity's nascent sense of self-in-relation grew to include fellowship, emotional bonds, social status, shared symbols of meaning, rigid customs, and the guidance of spiritual leaders. And these changes ultimately enabled the development of writing, organized government, architecture, mathematics, and the division of labor – all artifacts of relationship.

At this point, the concept of the separate individual with personal rights and freedoms did not yet exist. Instead, within the worldview of these civilizations, every person existed only as a member of some community, rather than perceiving themselves as independent individuals. For example, in his book *Freedom in the Making of Western Culture*, sociologist Orlando Patterson shows how attitudes about slavery reveal the state of individuality in any era. In Agrarian Era civilizations, slaves were owned collectively and their role was not economic, but social; they were kept as a means of strengthening the identity of the ruling community. "The antithesis of slavery in these societies was never freedom in the Western sense," Patterson continues. "Th[e] condition of belonging, of participating, of being protected by the community, constituted the ideal nonslave condition...."[39] As much as this is hard for us to understand or even imagine today from within our worldview of individual independence, Patterson is clear: "Personal freedom had no place in such societies."[40] Instead, identity was shaped solely by relationship and affiliation.

As we look at the various factors that defined and contributed to the Agricultural Era, then, we see that it isn't fully helpful to note only that people became agrarians during this era; *they did so as a function of their expanded sense of self-in-relationship.*

With all the benefits of this new perceptual framework, there were also unforeseen consequences. As professor of evolutionary psychiatry Bruce Charlton writes: "...animism continues to feature in people's beliefs and practices (after all animism remains the spontaneous mode of thought among all people, in all societies)...." But with the shift into a new mode of relating to the world, humans cease to perceive their unity with "*the whole significant world*, with the consequence that the world is no longer experienced as a whole.... Life becomes divided, and humans alienated."[41] In moving into relationship awareness, we lost some of our sense of belonging in the world, and with it some of the meaning in our lives. This sense of separation and isolation would only worsen in the era that followed, even as we gained tremendous advantages.

THE ERA OF DIVERGENCE

We first find clear evidence of the view of the individual as separate and distinct roughly three thousand years ago in ancient Greece, in what marks the beginning of the Modern Era. Population increase, migration and conquest had long added complexity to civilization, challenging the ability of the self-in-relationship perspective to guide people usefully. Imagine, for example, that you had always simply followed the time-honored traditions and habits of your tribe or community, but suddenly you were faced with interactions that weren't "covered" by those practices – insufficient crop yield, new types of people, unprecedented choices. For the first time, you would be forced to think for yourself.

In *The Unconscious Before Freud*, L.L. Whyte writes that during this time period:

...instinct and tradition having proved inadequate, the individual was being compelled to rely for guidance on his own mental processes.... Thus man became self-conscious. The individual became aware of his own thought.[42]

Sociologist Orlando Patterson supports this view, asserting that "a profound change in human thought" took place in ancient Athens, ushering in the concepts of individuality and rationality. On the basis of this shift in thought patterns, he explains that a complex economy of independent family farms and urban craftsmen and a democratic political state were created. These changes, along with a large population of slaves, emancipated the majority of people from economic and social dependency on a ruling class.[43] As a result, we see evidence of increasing individual contribution, giving rise to a modern civilization with incredible advances in technology, language, mathematics, warfare and architecture. *But the starting point was a change in thought.*

In ancient Rome, this trend continued and intensified, particularly with the rise of Christianity. Patterson reports on Christianity's role in the rise of the concept of individual freedom as it had never existed before:

[The Romans] refashioned the original religion of Jesus into their own image, making it the first, and only, world religion that placed [individual] freedom – spiritual freedom, redemption – at the very center of its theology. In this way, freedom was to be enshrined on the consciousness of all Western peoples; wherever Christianity took root, it garnered converts not only to salvation in Christ but to the ideal of [individual] freedom.[44]

With the fall of ancient Greece and Rome, individual divergence faltered for several centuries during the Middle Ages. Though the term "Dark Ages" has fallen out of use among historians, there is much evidence that the times truly were dark for much of the population of Western Europe, largely because of an inability to integrate divergent structures. For example, centralized political organization, literacy, specialized work, trade and export, and even plumbing were all generally lost.

But during this time, the seeds of individual divergence did not die; they merely lay dormant. With the Renaissance – a term that refers to the rebirth of classical Greek and Roman thought, and the individualism inherent therein – a new surge of divergence emerged.

In his book, *The Origins of European Individualism*, historian Aaron Gurevich tracks "the transition from earlier forms of community life, characterized by local, kinship groups and collective identity, towards a changed...society dominated by the cognitive, motivational individual." Though most historians place the rise of "the self-aware, autonomous European citizen" in the late fourteenth and fifteenth centuries, Gurevich argues that the origins of the movement can be traced to the 5th and 6th centuries. While this may be true, there is a clear surge in individualism from the 1300s to the 1500s spurred by the advent of printing, the spread of interest in lost ancient Greek thought, the Black Plague (which caused people to lose faith in the relational institution of the Church), and the Reformation, among other things.

In this latter example, the Reformation suggested that individuals could commune directly with God (without the Church as intermediary) and that their personal interpretation of the Bible was the final authority. Indeed, the New Testament itself supports individualist perceptions with its assertion that the individual soul has inherent value.[45]

This religious individualism eventually fueled the flame of political individualism, most notably in the writings of Thomas Hobbes, John Locke and later Jean-Jacques Rousseau and other French philosophers of the 18th century.[46] According to Rousseau's influential Social Contract theory, the state exists to serve the interests of the individuals, and individuals bear it no moral responsibility. The state simply represents the population's collective agreement to refrain from impinging on each other's freedoms. This is a sharp break from previous beliefs, in which the individual was thought to exist only as part of the community, with a clear moral obligation to serve society's interests.

These and similar individualist sentiments caught on and spread like wildfire, eventually driving the French and American revolutions, the US abolition of slavery, and industrial capitalism. As author, philosopher and professor Roger Scruton observes: "The history of Western society since the Enlightenment has been a history of emancipation, as individuals have freed themselves from the constraints imposed by social conventions and traditional roles."[47]

Fast forward to the present day, and we can see that the wave of divergence continued and, indeed, erupted wholesale with the Civil Rights movement, the Women's Liberation movement, the sexual revolution, the Gay/Lesbian Liberation Movement, student protests, decolonization, and the free speech movement. Each of these movements questioned conformity and promoted personal expression. And in each, a common thread was evident: what author James Farrell referred to as "the belief that politics and social institutions must respect (if not enhance) the inviolable dignity of persons (what Martin Luther King, Jr. called their 'somebodiness')."[48]

So, increasing divergence brought increasing freedom, creativity and personal expression. But as with the relationship-based worldview, there is a dark side to the divergent view. High levels of individualism come with high costs. As Geoff Mulgan, author of *Connexity: How to Live in a Connected World*, points out:

> It costs more if everyone travels in a private car and is willing to spend long spells in traffic jams; more if everyone chooses to live alone, or to live in a house large enough to accommodate the children of a previous marriage at weekends; more if people have to protect themselves against the actions of others that in another society might be held in check by mutual moral suasion.[49]

And while current levels of divergence are valuable and even necessary, they are harmful if not integrated into the whole of society. Our increasing social isolation has been well documented. Harvard professor Robert Putnam provides a wealth of telling statistics in his book *Bowling Alone*, asserting that "Our growing social-capital deficit threatens educational performance, safe neighborhoods, equitable tax collection, democratic responsiveness, everyday honesty, and even our health and happiness."[50]

Along the same lines, the General Social Survey (conducted across the United States in 1985 and 2004) found that the average respondent in 1985 reported having three confidants (people with whom they discussed important matters), whereas the average respondent in 2004 reported having no confidant. Such social isolation has been linked with increased crime and a decrease in democracy, as well as higher rates of mortality, morbidity, infection and depression.[51] Epidemiological studies first identified the link between social isolation and health risks, particularly coronary heart disease, in the 1970s and 1980s. According to the scholarly journal *Psychosomatic Medicine*: "The magnitude of risk associated with social isolation is comparable with that of cigarette smoking and other major biomedical and psychosocial risk factors."[52]

To understand how humanity might productively move forward from the current state of affairs, we must first understand that, for the purposes of living systems, divergent is not the same as separate. It is not sufficient for any one person in a human community simply to be different or distinct. That person's *contribution to the whole* must be different, *and* it must be integrated into the whole. Without such integration, that person risks being external to the living whole, which may in some way explain why isolation poses the health risks described above.

What is more, as levels of divergence reach critical levels, integration must occur or the whole system is put in jeopardy. When individual cells in our bodies diverge without integration, it is known as cancer. It seems our social context may be approaching just such a diagnosis: many have lost sight of the convergent whole and the web of relationship and pursue divergence for its own sake. This is particularly true in business, with its ethos of "constant growth for the sake of growth," without consideration of how it serves the living whole. If this divergence is not integrated into the whole, then the living system that is humanity – and ultimately the Earth – is jeopardized. And there is plenty of evidence of our precarious position in this regard.

Fortunately, there is also evidence that humanity is on the verge of a wave of rich integration.

THE ERA OF INTEGRATION

As divergence skyrocketed during the previous era, relationship also continued to grow more efficient, more personalized and more expansive. As Pierre Teilhard de Chardin noted in the mid-twentieth century:

Through the discovery yesterday of the railway, the motor car and the aeroplane, the physical influence of each man, formerly restricted to a few miles, now extends to hundreds of leagues or more. Better still: thanks to the prodigious biological event represented by the discovery of electromagnetic waves, each individual finds himself henceforth (actively and passively) simultaneously present, over land and sea, in every corner of the earth.[53]

More recently, radio, television, and telephone have been joined by computers, email and social media, facilitating fast, easy interaction. This trend will only accelerate and intensify, enabling more and more people to connect with each other. As Peter Russell notes in *The Global Brain*: "The interlinking of humanity that began with the emergence of language has now progressed to the point where information can be transmitted to anyone, anywhere, at the speed of light. Billions of messages continually shuttling back and forth, in an ever-growing web of communication, linking the billions of minds of humanity together into a single system."[54] It's a small world, after all.

And at the same time, people everywhere seem to be more and more aware of humanity's (and life's) vast convergence. Media and travel are helping us become aware of ourselves as "Humanity" – a living whole, not simply a collection of parts. As we untangle DNA, we find that we're not only more closely related to each other than we thought – we're also more closely related to other animals (and even plants!) than we imagined. The Gaia hypothesis paints a picture of all life on Earth as one cohesive organism.[55] And we're increasingly able to sense the impact of our actions on the rest of life, as well as the implications for us in the form of climate change and species extinctions.

So we've reached high levels of divergence, high levels of relationship and high levels of convergence. The result has been a predictable wave of integration. Twenty years after the social movements of the sixties, the Berlin Wall fell, breaking down an ideological and physical barrier to free-flowing integration of markets and communities. Since then, global media and ease of travel have steadily strengthened and tightened the web of social and economic connections. Financial markets have become more global and interconnected, facilitating interactions between traders, investors and banks. Deregulation of a range of industries has opened markets to competition, collaboration and participation by new players. Common markets like the European Union have integrated labor and trade. Worldwide, our lifestyles have become more closely tied to global fashion, food and entertainment trends. Where once there was strict division between academic disciplines, there is now a trend toward inter-disciplinary exploration and collaboration. And nowhere is the living, adaptive self-integrative property of our social context more evident than the Internet.

In a 2009 commencement speech at Portland University, environmentalist Paul Hawken observed that "[h]umanity is coalescing. It is reconstituting the world, and the action is taking place in schoolrooms, farms, jungles, villages, campuses, companies, refugee camps, deserts, fisheries and slums." The speech draws on Hawken's most recent book, titled: *Blessed Unrest: How the Largest Social Movement in History is Restoring Grace, Justice and Beauty to the World.* Hawken chronicles the large number of organizations and activities emerging in defense of the environment and social justice, noting that "we are part of the Earth's immune system each time we exercise our active compassion in the name of social justice and ecological health."[56]

Likewise, in 2008, Peter Senge and his co-authors offered *The Necessary Revolution: How Individuals and Organizations are Working Together to Create a Sustainable World.* The book is a collection of "inspiring stories from individuals and organizations tackling social and environmental problems around the globe." It describes how "ordinary people at every level are...working collaboratively across boundaries" to nurture the living whole.[57]

In each of these examples, there was no single driver or engineer, and there was nothing monolithic about the movements described. Instead, there was the self-organizing, self-integrative pattern of life, in all its divergence, relationship, convergence and resulting generativity.

Along the same lines, Robin Chase, founder of car-sharing company Zipcar, offers just one example of the evolution of business models toward increasing integration:

> Compare the phone you had as a kid to the one in your pocket now. The first was a telephone owned by a monopoly that you used at most only minutes a day. The latter is a smart networked device you refer to hundreds of times.

> The difference? First, the discovery of excess capacity. Imagine the wasted potential of a smartphone that could only play music and make and receive calls. Second, the creation of a platform. The creators of the mobile operating systems (Apple and Google, what I think of as INCs) figured out that they made *more* money when they opened up their rich and sophisticated platforms and allowed app developers to create value. Third, the ability of "Peers" – the small independent ecosystem, usually individuals and small companies – to aggressively scale and share ideas and assets: quirky, crafty, clever developers and users bringing their diverse selves to bear. Today, in less than seven years, we have over two million apps to choose from, and over 2 billion smartphone users.[58]

The idea of excess capacity – and a ready market of billions of customers – created convergent purpose, and the mobile operating systems created an infrastructure of relational space for millions of divergent app developers. Chase attributes these shifts to the Collaborative Economy, but it may be more accurate to think of it as the Integrative Economy, or even the Generative Economy or the Living Economy – an economy exhibiting the full set of living systems patterns, with resulting elegance and abundance.

In these ways, our social context reveals that what much of the world is *moving away from* is a divergent worldview – a primarily linear and reductionist way of engaging with the world. And what we're *moving toward* is an integrative perception – a holistic paradigm that brings together the individualistic worldview of the outgoing era, as well as the relational and convergent lenses that guided previous eras and that continue to guide some parts of the world today.

Although humanity seems to have one foot in an Era of Integration, with its promise of greater thriving, the transition is not guaranteed: most of all, it will require a significant dose of humility and open-mindedness on the part of the Western populations who have championed the divergent worldview for so long. As we become more aware of the shift we're participating in, the hope is that we will be able to move intentionally and quickly toward wiser, more fully life-honoring perspectives, so that together we may solve our most pressing environmental and social problems in time to avert the unthinkable.

2.4

THE EVOLVING BRAIN

THE PREVIOUS CHAPTERS presented evidence indicating that (1) era-level shifts occur because of evolutions in worldview, and (2) a new era-level shift is underway right now. So, why not stop there? Isn't an exploration of the brain going just a little too far down the rabbit hole?

Truly, this may be belaboring the point. (And if this is your feeling, you have my permission to skip ahead to the Section 3 and its exploration of the practice of thrivability.)

If we stop here, though, each of us is just so much flotsam being tossed about on the surging ocean of civilization. And not only is that a depressing, disempowering scenario - it's not the whole story. In the previous two chapters, we saw the view from above. But that's not where all the action is. At least as important is the drama taking place beneath the surface, at the level of the parts.

In living systems, the parts create the whole. Buckminster Fuller called the whole a "pattern integrity," life's ongoing capability to produce patterns from parts. His example was the human hand. All the cells in your hand are replaced every few years, he pointed out. The only static thing is life's ability to create the pattern that constitutes the marvel of that appendage. In this way, we see that a hand is not a constant thing but an ongoing process carried out by parts.

The same is true of our societies and organizations. It is the patterns formed by the thoughts and interactions of individual people that create the whole. Not only has it been the evolving thoughts and actions of individual people that ushered in the global changes of past eras; we're at it again. And this time, we have the opportunity to do it intentionally – but only with an understanding of changes taking place on an individual level.

With this in mind, this chapter will show that:

1. The structure of the human brain hasn't changed in 195,000 years.
2. We've gotten progressively better at *using* the brain we've always had.
3. A critical mass of people has started using – and understanding – the brain in a new way, and this is helping to usher in a new era.

1. THE STRUCTURE OF THE BRAIN HASN'T CHANGED IN 195,000 YEARS.

It may come as a great surprise to learn that the brain hasn't changed since the human species emerged on the scene. Scientists have determined from the shape and interior indentations of fossil skulls that the brains of early humans were physically the same as ours. In other words, the average Cro-Magnon man had the same brain structure as Einstein's.

Within this brain structure, neuroscientist Paul MacLean noted what he called the "triune brain":[59]

- The reptilian part (this area is dominant in reptiles) **guides convergent behavior.** Also called the brainstem and cerebellum, it is concerned with territory, possessions, and physical space. It repeats patterns and does not learn. It controls basic, instinctual behaviors, such as self-preservation and aggression.

- The mammalian part (or limbic section, that is like the brains of other mammals) **guides relationship with others and with context**. It includes the hypothalamus, hippocampus, and amygdala. It is concerned with status, emotions, competition, and the avoidance of pain and seeking of pleasure. It supports automatic control of body functions (including temperature and digestion), which enable the body to be in adaptive relationship with its environment, as well as value judgments and memory.

- The neo-cortex **enables divergent behavior**. Found only in mammals, it takes up two-thirds of the total brain mass of humans and has two sides:

  - The right side controls visual-motor, nonverbal, creative, abstract, musical and artistic functions. The mode of processing is rapid, complex, whole-pattern, spatial and perceptual.

  - The left side controls verbal, analytical, linear and rational functions, conscious thought and language.

- The whole brain is **self-integrating**, creating itself through relation to context, as well as through innovation.

If this has been the structure of the human brain for almost 200,000 years, how can we account for the different eras of human evolution, with their progressively increasing intellectual capabilities? If this progress was not the result of a physically evolving brain, then what was the cause?

2. WE'VE GOTTEN PROGRESSIVELY BETTER AT USING THE BRAIN.

The increasing ability to use the parts and patterns of the brain is not a physical trait passed on genetically, like the ability to hear or see. It is a cultural innovation, rather than a biological one. In other words, it is learned and passed on. Writes historian Ronald Wright in *A Brief History of Progress*:

The Old Stone Age now seems so remote.... Yet it ended so recently – only six times further back than the birth of Christ and the Roman Empire – that the big changes since we left the cave have all been cultural, not physical. A long-lived species like ours can't evolve significantly over so short an interval.[60]

What is more, there is reason to surmise that each evolutionary era corresponded with (and, indeed, can be defined by) the added ability to use one of the three parts of the brain.

For example, it's quite conceivable that in the Hunter-Gatherer Era, the reptilian section was the part of the brain used most, guiding humans to pursue security and survival. The mode of thinking was holistic and instinctive.

During the Agrarian Era, humans would have learned to draw more extensively on the mammalian part of the brain, as they pursued community and relationship. The mode of thinking was focused on recognition of patterns, cycles and connections.

And the Modern Era (including the Industrial Age) could very well have been made possible by our increasing ability to use both sides of the neo-cortex to analyze, synthesize and, most of all, diverge. The dominant mode of thinking was focused on parts, separateness, single answers to problems, linear cause-and-effect, and individual perspectives. Of course, there was art, with its right brain ability to synthesize, but the dominant mode in society has generally been analytical.

That developmental progression is theoretically repeated in every child born today. Normally developing newborns first learn to use the reptilian part (focused on wholeness, survival and instincts); then toddlers begin exercising the mammalian part (focused on relationship); and eventually preschoolers start using the neo-cortex (focused on the divergent self).

If early learning about brain use is not enabled, children remain arrested at a pre-modern stage, without self-awareness or speech. Conversely, historian Wright surmises that "a late-Paleolithic child snatched from a campfire and raised among us now would have an even chance at earning a degree in astrophysics or computer science."[61]

Of course, this isn't to say earlier civilizations were completely unable to use the neo-cortex. On the contrary, there is evidence of basic language, art and music as far back as the latter part of the Hunter-Gatherer Era. But in these earlier eras, we don't find innovation in art, music and other spheres to the degree it has existed since 1,000 BC (the starting point of the divergent Modern Era). Indeed, Wright explains, it took "100,000 years for a new style or technique to be developed" among Hunter-Gatherer humans.

What happened in 1,000 BC, then, to cause the most recent major shift in how people used their brains? In his landmark work, *The Origin of Consciousness and the Breakdown of the Bicameral Mind*, Julian Jaynes posited that the two sections of the neo-cortex operated independently ("bicamerally") until around 1,000 BC. Before that time, people were not capable of self-awareness – in other words, awareness of themselves as divergent individuals. Instead, the bicameral person was "ruled in the trivial circumstance of everyday life by unconscious habit...."

This created what Jaynes called, "fragility in the face of complexity." As cities grew in size and as migration brought intermingling of populations, bicameral civilizations were highly susceptible to collapse. Habit and instinct no longer sufficed.

Fortunately, humans rose to the challenge and developed the ability to operate the two sides of the brain "unicamerally." The true innovation of 1,000 BC, it seems, was ratcheting up our ability to use the neo-cortex more fully and effectively as the dominant brain structure of the times, with a resulting surge of divergent behavior.

Why is all this important for us now? Because it suggests we might be able to learn even more sophisticated ways of using the brain. And this may be our only means of salvation in the current circumstances (as it has been in every previous era-level shift).

3. A CRITICAL MASS OF PEOPLE IS STARTING TO USE - AND UNDERSTAND - THE BRAIN IN A NEW WAY, AND THIS IS HELPING TO USHER IN A NEW ERA.

At many (if not all) of the significant junctures in human history, increasing complexity compelled a few people to learn a new way of using their brains. This new learning was then passed on to others and again on to later generations. Eventually, a tipping point was reached, gradually affecting major populations of human civilization.

It seems we're approaching just such a pivot point in our own time. Specifically, it's quite plausible that the dawning Era of Integration is made possible by our increased ability to integrate all the parts of our brain into a fully coordinated whole.

One indication of this shift is the steady and dramatic rise of the average IQ since it was first tracked a century ago. According to a report in *American Scientist*, "[t]he average rate of increase seems to be about three IQ points per decade in the US...." An analysis of test scores in The Netherlands indicates an increase of an astonishing 35 points since the 1930s. This level of change has been found "on every major test, in every age range and in every modern industrialized country.... The increase has been continuous and roughly linear from the earliest days of testing to the present." What is particularly interesting is that the largest gains appear in abstract-reasoning that is not connected with particular school subjects or test-taking ability – and that is related to integrated brain functioning.

The *American Scientist* article confirms what we can guess instinctively: "These gains are far too rapid to result from genetic changes. There evidently are substantial environmental influences...." Again, our hunch is confirmed: "Modernization results in fundamentally different modes of thought."[62] In other words, as our lives have become more complex, we have had to adjust how we use the brain in order to be able to process the increasing input, stimulation and challenge we encounter.

The latest brain research adds to our understanding. "Intelligence relies not on one brain region or even the brain as a whole," reports neuroscience professor Aron Barbey. "Intelligence depends on the brain's ability to integrate information from verbal, visual, spatial and executive processes."[63] In other words, measurable increases in intelligence correspond with our growing ability to use the different parts of the brain in an integrated fashion.

There is even evidence that high levels of brain integration are correlated with achievement and success. For example, in one experiment, the brain activity of 33 Norwegian Olympic gold medalists was shown to be more integrated than that of 33 athletes who did not finish in the top ten.[64]

In fact, this phenomenon is not limited to the past hundred years, to test-taking scenarios or to elite athletes. History contains many early masters who have set an example of integrative thinking: people like Aristotle, Buddha, Jesus, Ralph Waldo Emerson, Thomas Jefferson, Albert Einstein, and Martin Luther King, Jr. Neurologist Jerre Levy of the University of Chicago had this to say about leaders like these:

> Great men and women of history did not merely have superior intellectual capacities within each hemisphere [of the brain]. They had phenomenal levels of emotional commitments, motivation, attentional capacity – all of which reflected the highly integrated brain in action.

Carl Sagan wrote about the emergence of "a new form of intellect." As evidence, he noted the rise of a "range of remarkably gifted multidisciplinary scientists and scholars." In fact, Sagan was a prime example himself. A biographer describes him as:

> A hyperpolymath conversant with astrophysics, biology, neuroscience, primate communication, atmospheric physics, geopolitics, nuclear strategy.... Sagan was the multidisciplinary scholar par excellence, the "Renaissance man" so uncommon in the age of specialization, of industrialized academia, where the divisions of labor are as real as in Henry Ford's factories.[65]

Another integrative thinker, Buckminster Fuller, summed up the situation cleverly: "Each age is characterized by its own astronomical myriads of new, special-case experiences and problems to be stored in freshly born optimum capacity human brains."[66]

Extraordinary individuals in history and modern-day multi-disciplinary pioneers have made their important contributions without any awareness of how they were using their brains. But new insights into the integrated brain may allow *us* to evolve actively and intentionally.

In particular, research is beginning to show that not only is integration of the different parts of the brain critical to intelligence, such integration relies on coordination with other sources of intelligence throughout the body. In fact, what we think of as "the brain" is taking on a fundamentally new meaning.

In the pioneering field of neuro-cardiology, for example, Dr. J. Andrew Armour revealed the heart as a functional brain in its own right. His research demonstrated that the heart has "a complex intrinsic neural network sufficiently sophisticated to qualify as a 'brain.'"

The heart's neural network meets all the criteria specified for a brain including several types of neurons, motor neurons, sensory neurons, interneurons, neurotransmitters, proteins and support cells. Its complex and elaborate neural circuitry allows the heart brain to function independently of the head brain and it can learn, remember, feel and sense.[67]

Not only that. In his landmark book, *The Second Brain*, neurobiologist and MD Michael Gershon shows that "the gut" also "contains a complex and fully functional neural network or 'brain.'" Through over a decade of research, Gershon has demonstrated that:

The gut brain, also known as the enteric brain, contains over 500 million neurons and sends and receives nerve signals throughout the chest and torso and innervates organs as diverse as the pancreas, lungs, diaphragm and liver. The gut brain is a vast chemical and neuro-hormonal warehouse and utilizes every class of neurotransmitter found in the head brain. Research has shown that the gut brain can learn, store memories and perform complex independent processing.[68]

Authors Grant Soosalu and Marvin Oka have conducted extensive research on the body's multiple brains, working to identify the "prime functions" of each, particularly in a leadership context. For example, they assert that the prime function of the head brain is creativity, drawing on cognition, analysis, synthesis, language, metaphor and narrative.

In comparison, they found that the heart brain is most associated with relational intelligence, processing the strength and quality of your relationships with others, your emotional responses, and the values that determine what is important to you and what your priorities are. Its prime function, they say, is compassion.

The gut brain draws on what Soosalu and Oka call "a deep and visceral sense of core self." It is where we draw on our instincts and what we might think of as collective intelligence. It guides our urge for safety and self-preservation. And it is the source of our will – of our gutsy determination. In these ways, the prime function of the gut brain is courage, say the two researchers.

Effective leadership calls for integrating all three prime functions, they report, which is why their work focuses on guiding leaders through intentional, thoughtful integration.

Indeed, a wide range of other studies have shown that we have a built-in mechanism for integration, without which our thoughtful intentions and efforts will be less than effective. Whole-body movement, including physical interaction and feedback, are vital to such integration of intelligence within each of the brains and across all of them. "It is through sensory input that the synapses in the brain multiply and actually build the ... mind," explained child development pioneer Maria Montessori.[69] The Institute for Neuro-Physiological Psychology reports similarly that "the experience of movement helps to build the architecture of the brain by strengthening pathways between nerves and association areas, which eventually provide a stable platform for coherent perception." In other words, movement, physical interaction and sensory feedback are critical to learning and the development of head-brain intelligence. It seems reasonable to assume this is true for heart and gut, as well – that our compassion and courage can only be fully developed through action and interaction. And there are indications that it is not just any type of movement that is needed for the highest levels of integration, but movement that is playful, expressive, delightful, sensorial, and engaging with beauty and nature – all of which help us connect with our fullest sense of aliveness.

Our built-in, whole-body integrating mechanism operates at another level, too. There is growing evidence that *every cell* has the characteristics and responsiveness of a brain... and even more remarkably, that *every molecule* responds to stimuli from the internal and external environments (including signals from the head, heart and gut brains). Pioneering physician and author Deepak Chopra describes this process:

> Biochemical messengers act with intelligence by communicating information, orchestrating a vast complex of conscious and unconscious activities at any one moment. This information transfer takes place over a network, linking all of our systems and organs, engaging all of our molecules ... as a means of communication. What we see is an image of a mobile brain – one that moves throughout our entire body located in all places at once and not just in the head.[70]

Thus, at both macro and micro levels, the entire body may be understood to be an integrative processing system. Signals from head, heart and gut brains are informed and integrated by what we might think of as the "whole-body" brain, which in turn informs and integrates them. Thus, we are coming to understand that it is not only the isolated, enclosed cerebral brain that enables intelligence; it is the combination of head, heart and gut brains, with vital ongoing input, guidance and integration by the whole-body brain.

With this, we see that those illustrious integrative thinkers from the past likely excelled at integrating the functions not only of their cerebral brains, but also of their heart, gut and whole-body brains. **They accessed and wove together creativity, compassion and courage as they acted and responded to life's call.**

In all, it seems that the fractal pattern of living systems has struck again, presenting itself not only within the head brain, but also across the whole body. We find a head brain that, most of all, guides us in understanding our distinct, **divergent** identity and in understanding the artifacts and patterns in the world around us; a heart brain that guides our **relationship** with others; a gut brain that gives us access to underlying instincts and insights – potentially from the whole of life - and that helps us find the courage and motivation to serve a **convergent** purpose larger than ourselves and larger than our own fears; and throughout the entire body, we find a **self-integrating**, self-organizing function that enables our highest, wisest form of intelligence to emerge.

As we come to understand the integrative nature of the whole-body brain, we are gradually changing how we parent and educate our children (incorporating music, movement and novelty, for example), how we stimulate discussion in work settings (inquiring first into what we care about most), how we make decisions (accessing each of the modes of intelligence), how we relate to our bodies (attuning to the signals we receive from heart and gut), and even how we live our lives (with greater movement, playfulness and connection with nature).

An uplifting, hopeful vision is emerging: with each new example set by an integrative thinker and each new method we apply to use our whole-body brains more fully, we take another step into the Era of Integration.

This prospect is particularly encouraging to us today. As we all bemoan the ever-increasing and overwhelming complexity in the world, we can find comfort in the thought that humans are capable of developing the intellect to handle it.

Still, it's too early to pour the drinks and put our feet up. We are at real risk of generating problems faster than even our whole-body brains can figure out how to solve them. And so there remains considerable urgency to our task.

2.5

An Emerging Level of Consciousness

THE FOURTH AND final "wall" in the matrix of how we understand reality is our individual consciousness – not the state of being awake and aware, but the underlying personal assumptions and filters that shape the reactions we choose, the way we relate to others, and the themes that preoccupy us.

In a general sense, this is what we typically think of as our level of maturity. And it is the realm of consciousness that can be observed and assessed. You know a three-year-old struggling for independence when you see one, just as the grace of elderly wisdom is plain to see. In fact, distinct stages or levels have been identified, with each level representing a characteristic "frame of reference or lens" through which individuals perceive and react to their social world. And reliable assessment methods have been formulated to ascertain a person's current stage of consciousness.*

The premise of this chapter is that a critical mass of people has moved into a new stage characterized by *integration* of the previously dominant levels of maturity, in a powerful meshing of universal instincts and intuition, community orientation, and individual achievement. And as these people progress, they are introducing cultural

---

* In reality, a person is not simply *at* one level; though we spend most of our time at one level, occasionally we rise above it and occasionally we fall back to a previous level, depending on our circumstances. For this reason, some scholars refer to a person's "center of gravity."

artifacts that invite others to follow in their footsteps, raising the bar of society in general and ushering in a new era.

When you think about it, such a correlation between individual and societal progression makes sense: acquiring society's dominant worldview is the goal of socialization and defines what it means to be a functional adult. If the majority of the population is at a certain stage of individual development, then that society's core values, practices and artifacts will guide new generations to that stage of development and no further. For example, today's dominant Western value of individualism is reinforced by the educational system, the way economic development is channeled and measured, the popular media and our social customs and mores.

Naturally, there will be a small number who will progress further as a result of their personal circumstances or of their own initiative. They will gradually be joined by more, until eventually their numbers reach some critical mass that begins to influence the overarching values, practices and artifacts of society. And eventually, induction into society extends to the next level of development.

It is in this way that human consciousness and civilizations progress. As with use of the brain, consciousness is learned, not passed on genetically. Although children born today necessarily start at the lowest level of maturity, they don't have to struggle in isolation to make their way through each stage. They have access to the examples of parents and teachers and of society's surrounding context of rules and norms. They are able to absorb in childhood the lessons that took previous generations lifetimes to learn. The speed with which they progress through the spectrum depends almost entirely on the stage and artifacts of their community. A child born into an integrative civilization would presumably progress quickly to that level.

The chart on the following page shows the clear parallels between the prevailing theories about stages of consciousness and those regarding societal development. Individually or collectively, humans seem to travel along a distinct path toward maturity. Though the terminology is different across the various theories, there is a consistent progression from an initial stage focused on universal instincts, to one focused on

A Comparison of Theories of Collective and Individual Progression

Eras (traditional)	Hunter-Gatherer	Agrarian	Modern/Industrial	(no consensus on this era's name)	
Eras (revised)	Convergence	Relationship	Divergence	Integration	
"Triune" brain	Reptilian	Mammalian	Neo-cortex	Integration	
Stages of human lifecycle	Infancy	Childhood	Teen Years	Adulthood	Maturity
Abraham Maslow	Physiological Survival & Safety	Love & Belonging	Self-Esteem	Self-Actualization	Self-Transcendence
Jane Loevinger	Impulsive/Self-Protective	Conformist	Self-Aware/Conscientious/Individualistic/Autonomous	Integrated	
Jean Gebser	Magic	Mythical	Mental	Integral	
Spiral Dynamics	Instinctive-Survivalistic	Magical - Animistic	Egocentric-Narcissistic/Purposeful-Authoritarian/Scientific Modernism	Communitarian-Egalitarian	Integrative/Holistic
Robert Kegan & Lisa Lahey		Socialized Mind	Self-Authoring Mind	Self-Transforming Mind	
Paul Ray		Traditional	Modern	Creative	
Sigmund Freud	Id	Superego	Ego		
Carl Jung	Collective Unconscious	Collective Consciousness	Personal Conscious & Unconscious	Self/Integration	

relationships, to another focused on individual, mental achievement and differentia-tion, to a fourth stage focused on an integration and inclusive transcendence of all previous stages.

There is no judgment inherent in the hierarchical presentation of stages; each is appropriate and effective in certain contexts. And though we may seem to progress along a clear path, the work of each stage is not completed with the first pass through; we spend the rest of our lives returning to each stage, as if in a continuously spiraling pattern, to deepen our mastery of the full spectrum of consciousness. Importantly, "wise" people – i.e., those with greater ability to integrate the whole spectrum – tend to thrive more; that is, their lives seem to be marked by abundant joy, insight, ease and fluid, uplifting relationships.

Although the stages parallel the progression from childhood through to adult-hood, it is also critical to note that not all adults make the full journey. Currently, the majority of Western adults seem to be centered at the individualistic stage that defined the Modern (and Industrial) Era.

In one of the theories represented, developmental psychologist Abraham Maslow famously offered his take on the stages of human consciousness more than fifty years ago. At the peak of his Hierarchy of Needs (first released in 1954) is a level he called self-actualization. This level differs from the preceding and more individualistic self-esteem in its greater emphasis on contribution and impact. In later writings, Maslow split that highest level into two, adding the need for what he termed "transcendence."[*] Though he uses his own terms, the gist of his theory is that at the highest level of de-velopment, people are driven by the need to find their best form of divergence and their best relationships to their surrounding context, all with the goal of transcending themselves through creativity and problem solving. This, we now know, is the pattern of all living things.

---

[*] It is somewhat telling that these later writings have not entered the mainstream understanding of Maslow's work. His expanded theory lies beyond the dominant divergent consciousness.

In his 1975 work, *Man's Ultimate Search for Meaning*, psychiatrist and Holocaust survivor Victor Frankl supported Maslow's fuller theory:

> The true meaning of life is to be found in the world rather than within man or his own psyche, as though it were a closed system.... Human experience is essentially self-transcendence rather than self-actualization. Self-actualization is not a possible aim at all, for the simple reason that the more a man would strive for it, the more he would miss it.... In other words, self-actualization cannot be attained if it is made an end in itself, but only as a side effect of self-transcendence.[71]

Carl Jung also shared Maslow's belief in the importance of divergent self-actualization, which he termed "individuation." At the same time, like Maslow in his later writings, he stressed the importance of striving for integration, unity and wholeness.[72] According to David Wulff, author of *The Psychology of Religion*, Jung asserted that the purpose of life is "...an unending process of differentiation and integration that repeats itself on ever higher planes," a process which Jung called the "transcendent function."[73] According to another overview of the famed psychoanalyst's theories, "Jung perceived the *primary* motivating force to be spiritual in origin. It was from the soul that the complementary drives of differentiation and integration arose, fueling the processes of growth, development, and healing."[74] Again, this seems to be a different way of describing the ubiquitous pattern of all living things.

Though not all theories recognize the similarity between individual and societal progression, two stand out in this regard. In the 1950s, cultural philosopher Jean Gebser stated that the major eras of human civilization were stages of evolution in consciousness. He interpreted the turmoil of the two world wars as evidence of the failure of one structure of consciousness alongside the emergence of another, which he termed "integral." As proof, Gebser documented transformations in almost every major field: architecture, fine arts, anthropology, literature, political science, communication theory, mass communication, social movements, psychology, and philosophy. In particular, he noted the inclusion of time in physics as an example of expanded consciousness and its impact on society.

Similarly, the Spiral Dynamics theory tracks progression of consciousness along a series of stages. Developed by psychologists Don Beck and Christopher Cowan, based on the earlier work of Clare Graves, the theory implicitly applies to individuals, communities and civilizations.

If there is general agreement among some of the most respected theorists about the existence of an integrative level of consciousness, what, then, is the view from this level? What are the defining characteristics of the integrative worldview it represents?

A Consciousness of Divergence

The first defining characteristic of this level of consciousness is the ability to hold and consider multiple **divergent perspectives** at one time. According to developmental psychologist Susanne Cook-Greuter, people at this level "can take multiple points of view and shift focus effortlessly among many states of awareness."[75] This can mean several things:

- They are more tolerant of and open to diverse perspectives. In our times, this has been supported by increasing education, travel, exposure to global media, and globalization. Similarly, people at this level are more aware and accepting of varying individual personality types. The popularity of personality assessments like the Myers-Briggs Type Indicator (MBTI) has introduced millions of people to the concept that, as one popular book title asserts, "I'm not crazy, I'm just not you." In these ways, people at an integrative level of consciousness are more open than the previous level to the wide diversity of humanity. In a way, this may be considered a rediscovery of existing wisdom: according to Princeton University professors Robert Jahn and Brenda Dunn, some Native American and East Asian cultures believe that one cannot fully understand a situation until at least seven points of view have been considered.[76]

- People at an integrative level of consciousness are able to embrace opposing or paradoxical concepts, whereas earlier levels are more likely to be limited to a black-or-white, right-or-wrong view. In his book *Opposable Minds*, best-selling author Roger Martin consistently observed this ability among highly effective leaders. In a process he calls "integrative thinking," Martin describes how "without panicking or simply settling for one alternative or the other, they're able to produce a synthesis that is superior to either opposing idea."[77] In this way, people at this level are likely to demonstrate both wisdom and novelty in their approach to problems.

- Those using greater integrative consciousness understand and acknowledge the full path of human development, embracing rather than rejecting the teenager's push for independence or the co-worker's need for affirmation, for example. According to philosopher Ken Wilber in an explanation of the Spiral Dynamics theory, the earlier levels of consciousness are marked by the belief that their respective worldviews are the only correct perspectives. Within the emerging stage of consciousness, "one can, for the first time, *vividly grasp the entire spectrum of interior development*, and see that each level...is crucially important...." (italics original)[78]

A Consciousness of Relationship

The second major defining characteristic of the integrative worldview is recognition that **life is a dynamic process** of relationship and reaction.

This goes beyond simply recognizing the network effect in an interconnected world. More than previous levels, this worldview pays attention to principles, patterns and processes of learning and becoming, without necessarily losing sight of single parts and static moments in time. It recognizes the ongoing flow and resilience of life. And it celebrates the opportunity to contribute to evolution along the way, as integrative thinkers consider themselves "human becomings" more than human beings. As

Buckminster Fuller mused: "I am not a thing – a noun. I seem to be a verb, an evolutionary process – an integral function of the universe."[79]

Thus, according to Cook-Greuter, people at this level "feel embedded in nature – birth, growth and death, joy and pain – are seen as natural consequences, patterns of change in the flux of time."[80] Maslow noticed that people at an integrative level find the journey as important as the goal. And whereas the previous worldview left us feeling isolated and frantic – measuring our success moment by moment in purely tangible terms of success or failure – the integrative worldview brings back in vogue the saying, "Go with the flow," not meaning to be carried along by the crowd or the current but instead meaning to align our actions with the larger flow and pattern of life.

A Consciousness of Convergent Wholeness

The third defining characteristic of this worldview is awareness of the **convergent unity of all life**.

Whereas the previous level sees things as either separate or united, people at an integrative level of consciousness are able to hold the paradox of individuality within unity, of seeing the whole without losing sight of the contingent parts. Just as the Gaia theory posits that the Earth is one immense self-regulating organism, integrative thinkers sense that we are all integral parts within a larger set of living systems. Maslow called this "unitive consciousness." And Cook-Greuter observes that "feelings of belongingness and feelings of one's separateness and uniqueness are experienced without undue tension...."[81]

Albert Einstein described such a view in one of my favorite examples of integrative thinking:

A human being is a part of the whole, called by us "Universe," a part limited in time and space. He experiences himself, his thoughts and feelings as something separated from the rest – a kind of optical delusion of his consciousness.

This delusion is a kind of prison for us, restricting us to our personal desires and to affection for a few persons nearest to us. Our task must be to free ourselves from this prison by widening our circle of compassion to embrace all living creatures and the whole of nature in its beauty.[82]

Environmentalist John Muir made a similar observation: "When we try to pick up anything by itself, we find it hitched to everything else in the universe."[83]

And Argentinean writer Jorge Luis Borges thoughtfully reflected, "I am not sure that I exist, actually. I am all the writers that I have read, all the people that I have met, all the women that I have loved; all the cities that I have visited, all my ancestors."[84]

This recognition of infinite divergence within total convergence invites high levels of compassion: people at this level sense that what happens to you also affects me because we are integral parts of the same living system, like two cells within the same body, each nourished by the same spark of life.

A CONSCIOUSNESS OF SELF-INTEGRATION

This brings us to the fourth defining characteristic: attunement to the **will and wisdom present in all living systems**.

This characteristic represents the most significant departure yet from the previous level of consciousness, with its focus on the authority and independence of the individual, on the purely tangible, and on the central nervous system as the sole possible repository of volition and intelligence. To the individualistic level of consciousness, the idea of being an integral part of a larger, intention-filled living system is anathema, smacking of the communal religious and magical views of earlier levels, in which the individual is unquestioningly subordinate to an all-powerful and little understood "higher power."

But unlike earlier conformist worldviews, the integrative view has little to do with organized religion; it is informed by rigorous and open (even scientific) inquiry; and it honors individual motivation and judgment just as fervently as it does the will and wisdom of the larger encompassing systems.

The emerging view is based in part on the observation that, within the hierarchy of any living system, each level of life displays greater intelligence than the levels beneath it as an emergent result of the pooled efforts and capabilities of the parts. Atoms form molecules, which form cells, which form organs and bones, which form bodies, which contain nervous systems that enable the conscious intelligence of the mind. Each successive level has greater capabilities than the previous. According to the integrative worldview, the ubiquitous nested pattern of life does not end with our minds or brains. Instead, there is much evidence that this pattern extends to the levels of our organizations and communities and indeed to all humanity, and that collective intelligence increases at each progressive stage – intelligence that is in some ways available to the component parts.

This view is more than just an extended version of "two heads are better than one." It is also recognition of the underlying order and elegance inherent at every level of the universe. It is not only progressively aggregated intelligence going up the hierarchy; it's also recognition of a deeper level of self-organization at the very core of the hierarchy. It harkens back to the etymology of the word consciousness, which means "knowing with."

At a basic level, this calls for trusting your gut, following your instincts, pausing to reflect before making a decision – something all of us do on a regular basis. With an integrative level of consciousness, we find another level of intentionality, as we "tune in" in whatever manner suits us in order to discover the most natural, appropriate way forward in any situation. It's listening for what's truly needed, with awareness that wisdom is available from life itself. It's attunement to beauty, elegance and grace as signs of the rightness of a course of action.

This corresponds with Jung's concept of the collective unconscious. "In addition to the personal unconscious generally accepted by medical psychology," he also noted "the existence of a second psychic system of a universal and impersonal nature."[85] To him, this was the source of our instincts and urges, as well as of the universal symbols that appear in our dreams. According to Jung, "the multiplicity of the empirical world rests on [this] underlying unity."*

Psychology professor George Boeree relates Jung's assertions to the Hindu view that:

> Our individual egos are like islands in a sea: We look out at the world and each other and think we are separate entities. What we don't see is that we are connected to each other by means of the ocean floor beneath the waters.[86]

Did Jung believe this unified realm exhibited will and wisdom? Consider synchronicity. Defined by Jung as "an acausal connecting principle," synchronicity is a term he coined to explain "a governing dynamic that underlies the whole of human experience and history."[87] To him, the collective unconscious exhibited order and intention conveyed in the form of instincts, urges, symbols and signs. He spent most of his career collecting and studying examples of what he called "causeless order" or "meaningful orderedness."

And did Jung consider these synchronistic experiences characteristic of a certain type of psychological development? Though such experiences can happen for anyone, he observed that people with an integrative orientation of consciousness are more likely to be attuned to the collective unconscious and alert to its "connecting" and "governing" indications. Jung called this stage "self-realization," a concept almost identical to Maslow's self-actualization and transcendence. To him, the hallmark of this stage is the integration of individual consciousness (or ego) with the collective unconscious. This did not mean the ego or individual personality is given up; it meant the individual finds his or her unique place within the whole. They find their groove.

To Jung, this constituted a new spirituality, apart from religion: the belief – or, more accurately, the *awareness* – that we are an active and indivisible part of something

---

* If this seems similar to concepts from quantum mechanics, it's no coincidence: Jung spent time with Einstein and Wolfgang Pauli.

larger than our individual egos, something that provides inherent order and direction and that invites a sense of meaning, wonder, compassion and beauty.

Many other developmental psychologists have shared this view. For example, Maslow's self-transcendence stage explicitly included spirituality. Though he often referred to it as religion, in his 1976 book *Religions, Values and Peak Experiences*, Maslow asserts:

> I want to demonstrate that spiritual values have naturalistic meaning, that they are not the exclusive possession of organized churches, that they do not need supernatural concepts to validate them, that they are well within the jurisdiction of a suitably enlarged science, and that, therefore, they are the general responsibility of all mankind.[88]

In particular, his study of successful people explored peak experiences, which, to him, were spiritual experiences. Maslow believed such experiences "transport us out of ordinary consciousness into a higher dimension of being, providing us with glimpses of a transcendent reality and allowing us to touch ultimate values such as truth, beauty, goodness and love." His interest in these kinds of experiences grew so great that he helped found the field of transpersonal psychology, which, according to the *Journal of Transpersonal Psychology*, "is concerned with the study of humanity's highest potential, and with the recognition, understanding, and realization of unitive, spiritual, and transcendent states of consciousness."[89]

In all, the integrative level of consciousness recognizes the will and wisdom of the whole of life, as well as the opportunity to be conscious, divergent participants in its flow and pattern. In contrast to the powerlessness of earlier deterministic religious views, the integrative worldview is active and experimental, with a strong evolutionary urge.

Tom Atlee, founder of the Co-Intelligence Institute, concurs: "Our emerging crises are a call to become wiser, collectively – to become the deep collective wisdom and monumental creativity of evolution, itself, becoming conscious through us.... To become evolution is to say, 'We are Life, I am Life, itself, finding ways to live, ways that work for and nurture Life.'"[90]

Similarly, futurist Barbara Marx Hubbard calls people at the integrative stage "Universal Humans," those who are "connected through the heart to the whole of life, attuned to the deeper intelligence of nature, and called forth irresistibly by spirit to creatively express his or her gifts in the evolution of self and the world."[91]

In these ways, we see that the integrative worldview warrants its name, bringing together previous views in the typical, ever-transcendent pattern of all living systems.

The ongoing shift to integrative consciousness is as monumental as the one that took place when we learned from Copernicus that we weren't at the center of the Universe. Now, we learn we're also *not separate* from the rest of the Universe – we're interwoven within it and an integral and creative part of it. Instead of Descartes' "I think, therefore I am," the new era's theme might be, "I live, therefore I seek to transcend." And there is much evidence to believe that the pattern of converge, connect, diverge and integrate will be our means.

Why is all of this important?

Because rising to this worldview is humanity's best means of addressing our escalating global environmental and social challenges. Informed by multiple perspectives and choosing from the full spectrum of available reactions and choices, the integrative worldview is fundamentally a wiser one. And the more we are able to tap into the intelligence of all humanity, and indeed of all life – in its full divergence, in the collective wisdom of its convergence and in the beauty and elegance of its self-integration - the more likely we are to find creative, adaptive solutions to our complex problems.

Physicist Ervin Laszlo shared this view:

Einstein was right: the problems created by the prevalent way of thinking cannot be solved by the same way of thinking. This is a crucial insight. Without renewing our culture and consciousness we will be unable to transform today's dominant civilization and overcome the problems generated by its shortsighted mechanistic and manipulative thinking.... The conscious orientation of the next cultural mutation – the shift to a new civilization – depends on the evolution of our consciousness. This evolution has become a precondition of our collective survival.[92]

As far back as 1949, Jean Gebser said it even more bluntly: "Either we will be disintegrated and dispersed, or we must resolve and effect integrality."[93]

Either we will move resolutely in the direction of wisdom and compassion, embracing our ability and opportunity to cultivate thriving for all life, or we will regress to more barbaric ways of understanding and interacting.

"How good a society does human nature permit?" asked Maslow. Perhaps the more appropriate question, posed by a group of scientists and authors of the book, Limits to Growth, is: "How good a human nature does society permit?"[94] The task, then, is to give a deliberate upward nudge to the bar society uses to induct its members into their shared reality.

SECTION 3

COMMITTING TO THE PRACTICE OF THRIVABILITY

3.1

CUE THRIVABILITY

THE PREVIOUS SECTION of this book opened with a revised story from science, offering interesting new insights – prime among them that *there is life* (!) and that it operates in specific ways that we can participate in and cultivate. Not only that: the subsequent chapters showed that we have unwittingly been participating in life's patterns *all along*, as individuals, as communities and as a species.

As we've seen, this is more significant than it may appear. In the outgoing era, life was not fully acknowledged, and thriving wasn't even on the radar. Instead, competing, consuming and efficiency dominated our attention. In contrast, the new era reminds us that we're vibrantly, dynamically alive and that thriving *is* possible – and actually necessary. This emerging era shows us that competing, consuming and efficiency are, indeed, part of the story, but by far not the most important parts. It reveals to us that our own thriving is tied up with all other life thriving. And it offers a basic recipe for cultivating "thrivability" – the ongoing ability of life to thrive at every level within a living system.

So, while it is true (as the previous chapters have shown) that the incoming era is characterized by integration (the fourth part of the living systems recipe), perhaps a more meaningful name for this new phase of human evolution is not the Era of Integration but the Age of Thrivability. After all, integration is not truly the point. For fans of Ken Wilber's Integral Theory, the point is not to "be Integral." Getting caught up in only the patterns (or in any one of them) brings to mind the Buddhist admonition not to look at the finger pointing at the moon and mistake it for the moon. Instead, **we need to integrate as a means to cultivate thrivability.**

Similarly, advocates of change and innovation may also benefit from such clarity of focus. The goal is not to manage change or to innovate, nor is it to improve connectivity, to have a "smart" city or to be agile. It is not to create new jobs, to attract investment or to dedicate a section of town to innovation or the arts or entrepreneurship. Though these things may be useful, they are a means to a larger end. Whatever our occupation or industry, **the real point of our efforts is to participate in and support life's ongoing ability to thrive.**

This clarity helps us aim sufficiently high. It prompts us to ask big enough questions. It encourages us to look beyond habitual patterns of thought and action, and beyond existing infrastructures and institutions to see new possibilities. It invites us to cultivate all the fertile conditions that are needed: **divergent expression and contribution; dynamic, responsive relationship; convergent identity enlivened by collective action; and the animating spark of self-integration.**

The preceding section of this book ended with an appeal to give an upward nudge to the way society inducts people into a shared reality. Such induction happens in our collective spaces – in schools, in community, in businesses, in families. These are our practice grounds for living out the dominant paradigm. Therefore, this next section of the book will focus on what we can do in these shared spaces – and primarily within our organizations – to induct people (starting with ourselves!) into a shared reality characterized by a broad commitment to thrivability.

In fact, what is truly needed is broad commitment to enabling life to thrive *over time to ever expanding degrees.* After all, the ability to thrive is not a static end goal or an absolute, ideal state. Instead, it is an unfolding that holds all the cycles of life, including periods of death, decay and renewal. It demands a continuous assessment and adjustment based on emerging insights and evolving conditions. It calls for an ever-advancing inquiry, asking: "What is the wisdom needed in this moment, within these circumstances, to support life's ongoing ability to thrive?" And it is a purposeful set of responsive actions.

Seb Paquet, global curator of ideas, connector of people and co-catalyst at the innovative Enspiral network of companies, shares his perspective on this dynamic nature:

> Thrivability is a philosophy of work that is centered on performing actions that are generative. This is in contrast to sustainability. Something is sustainable if you can keep doing it forever; I associate sustainability with circles, going round and round. But I associate thrivability with spirals. Something that is thrivable will spiral out, constantly improving, becoming more beautiful or cleaner or more enjoyable, and often all of these at once. It is a continual unfolding.[95]

With this in mind, there is value in exploring what it means to have not only a *commitment* to thrivability but an ongoing and ever-unfolding *practice* of thrivability. This is what the following chapters will explore.

3.2

THE LIVING ORGANIZATION

THE STARTING POINT in our exploration of the practice of thrivability is to make sure we have a good understanding of what we're working with – a living organization. To that end, this chapter will first revisit the four living systems patterns as they are present in our organizations, offering a working model we can carry forward. It will then address several common "conceptual stumbling blocks" that can make it difficult to fathom an organization as, literally, "alive."

In revisiting the living systems patterns in an organizational context, the metaphor of a tree offers useful guidance. It gives us a way of thinking about an organization holistically and dynamically, highlighting how the patterns work together. It helps us recognize how those patterns are present at any scale, from the mom-and-pop shop to the multinational corporation. And it offers additional clues about how we can cultivate the conditions of thrivability in our organizations.

- **Divergent Parts:** At the base of the tree, we can imagine that the roots represent the different people in the organization, with their many talents, interests and perspectives. A tree needs a broad, divergent root base both to have access to different sources of nutrients and to be able to support the weight of the trunk and branches. Similarly, an organization hoping to thrive

and adapt over time needs the diverse contributions and perspectives of the people working
within it.

It is at the level of the roots that life first
flows into the tree, just as life enters the
organization through the living people
who comprise it. In our organizations,
then, the challenge is to invite and cultivate as much of that life as possible, so that
people bring the best of themselves to the
workplace and are nourished in the process. In
other words, the ongoing opportunity is to engage
the **Passion** of the people working within the organization.

- **Convergent Wholeness:** At the top of the tree, we can imagine the branches, leaves and fruit represent the organization's offering out into the world – its shared, convergent **Purpose**. After all, people generally come together in organization to make some collective contribution to a customer or community. *Without* that shared purpose, they are just a crowd, serving merely as context for each other. *With* a convergent purpose, the organization can take on a life of its own, remaining coherent and consistent over time – even as individual people come and go – and demonstrating new characteristics and capabilities previously not present at the level of the individual alone.

Just as the tree raises up its leaves to receive light and life from the sun, an organization extends its offering out into the world in order to receive life in the form of relationships with customers and community, along with money or other forms of value. Here, then, the task is to ensure that the Purpose is, indeed, convergent – that it is shared and compelling for those within the organization and that it engages those being served, inviting and nurturing as much of their "life" as possible. The opportunity is to ensure that the offering represents a valuable contribution to everyone involved – and if the organization is to enjoy full thrivability, then the definition of "valuable" must encompass not only tangible benefit but also intangible values like a deepening sense of community and meaning.

- **Patterns of Relationship:** Connecting the top and bottom of the tree is the trunk. This is the equivalent of an organization's infrastructure – the buildings, equipment, processes, practices and agreements that support and connect the flow of life and work throughout an organization.

Traditionally, we have considered the infrastructure to be the full extent of the organization, with employees, customers and community (not to mention the biosphere) thought to be external to the organization. Business schools have taught us that an organization is nothing more than a processing machine – like some kind of old fashioned meat grinder – with people and other resources fed into one end of the mechanism and products and services spilling out the other end into the arms of waiting customers.

Instinctively, we know that this understanding is incomplete and deeply problematic on many levels. In particular, the mechanistic view of organizations as machines prompts us to put people in service of infrastructure and process – the very definition of bureaucracy. The purpose of the work becomes filling out paperwork, sitting in meetings, operating the production line – in other words, keeping the machine running. Inevitably, the infrastructure becomes stagnant and bloated, the passion and life get sucked out of us, and the organization's offering grows uninspiring at best and toxic at worst.

Fortunately, our tree metaphor suggests an alternate perspective and a different path. It may come as a surprise to learn that the vast majority of the connective, supportive trunk of a mature tree is dead. Only a thin layer of living tissue called the cambium is alive, resting just under the bark and transporting nutrients from roots to leaves and transferring the energy of the sun from leaves to roots. Though most of the trunk is dead, it performs a vital function – it lifts the leaves up and out to the sun. In the same way, we can recognize that the infrastructure of an organization provides vital support and connection, enabling work to get done and allowing an offering to be extended out into the world. But importantly, we can also recognize that the infrastructure is the *non-living* part of the organization. This insight not only helps us keep infrastructure in its proper place – in service of Purpose and Passion, rather than the other way around. It also opens the door to reimagining every aspect of infrastructure, molding it to cultivate vital qualities of thrivability, like human connection, inspiration and responsiveness. Think, for example, about the revolutionary design of Apple stores: instead of forcing customers to line up at a cash register, the cash register is brought to them in the form of small handheld devices. No aspect of infrastructure is allowed to get in the way of human relationship and what Apple calls the "transformational experience."

When infrastructure is clearly in service of the life in an organization, what naturally emerges is what I call **Practical Play**. Play doesn't just bring about the experience of joy – one indication that we are thriving; it's also how we learn, collaborate and innovate best. We have mistakenly assumed that play is the opposite of work. But the reality is that play is the way work gets done most effectively. In designing infrastructure, then, the question becomes: what is our playground and what are the rules of our game?

What we are talking about here is not frivolous play – it is supremely practical, in clear service of our goals. In addition to designing supportive and connective infrastructure, the spirit of Practical Play is about adopting a stance and a mindset of curiosity, joyful connection and alignment with life in the interest of effective flow.

- **Self-Integration:** Returning to our tree metaphor, life flows into and through a tree naturally and effortlessly. The process is self-integrating and self-organizing. For us, the implication is that our own role in organizations can be reconceived from operators of a machine to gardeners, farmers – **stewards**, even – creating the fertile conditions for life's natural processes to unfold. This means tending to divergent parts, convergent wholeness and patterns of relationship, setting the stage for life's innate tendency to self-integrate. And in collective human endeavors such as organizations and communities, it also means creating conditions for the spark and spirit of life – the human spirit – to shine through and to be renewed through beauty, inspiration, meaning, nature, art and celebration.

To put the tree metaphor to the test, think about an organizational or community context you've experienced – a place where you work, a store you frequent, a family gathering or a community meeting – and reflect on where these patterns are well cultivated and where they're not. To what degree is every person involved able to express themselves, share their gifts, and be nourished at multiple levels? To what extent do people feel united by a shared sense of identity, purpose and collective action? How well do infrastructure and interactions support the flow of collaboration – and even the flow of meaning and life? How well are all of these things in alignment and coherence? Where and when are beauty, celebration, play and renewal present in support of life's animating spark?

In all, the tree metaphor helps us see that our organizations are made up not *only* of infrastructure. Clearly, an organization is the entire living system of infrastructure <u>and</u> the employees with their life-filled passion and unique talents and perspectives, <u>and</u> customers, who hold many wide-ranging interests, needs and desires, along with the purpose that engages all of them. It <u>is</u> the individual people who work there and the customers and community who engage with them. It <u>is</u> the dynamic process and pattern of interaction in between. And it <u>is</u> an emergent level of life with its own interests, needs and goals. It is *all* of those things at once. Part of the practice of stewardship, then, is developing the ability to hold and navigate the often challenging paradox of that complex reality.

Seeing the organization as one coherent living system then opens up new possibilities. For example, it has long been known (and verified by botanists) that the branch system of a tree is a rough mirror image of its root system. Similarly, there is power in exploring how the fundamental aspects of what engages customers can be mirrored in what engages employees, so that teachers come alive with their own learning, health care workers feel nourished toward optimum wellness, and so on.

As we emerge from the mechanistic era, grasping all of this can be challenging. We struggle to see the life in our organizations when they lack the concrete form of a tree or of a human body. We strain to sense their self-organization when we typically feel such control over them. Following are some of the most common sticking points related to viewing organizations as living systems, along with my responses, which first appeared in a blog post entitled, "It's Alive!" These insights may be useful to carry forward into subsequent chapters, as well as into your own practice of thrivability.

Objection #1: It's just a metaphor – don't get carried away. The resistance here is that if we take any metaphor as literal truth, then we start to apply it blindly and inappropriately as a one-size-fits-all prescription. And every metaphor has its limits.

It should be clear by now that I understand the living systems view not as a metaphor but as a literal definition. And that's important. Within the dominant mechanistic view of organizations, sustainability and corporate social responsibility are awkward add-ons that don't naturally fit, and so they generally bounce out or are implemented half-heartedly. With a living systems view, though, those elements are inherently part of the organizational DNA. When we see organizations as living ecosystems, the goal more naturally shifts to enabling life to thrive – contributing to and participating in life's process and pattern. The most logical activities become those that support the fertile conditions for thriving at multiple levels (individual, organizational, customer, community, biosphere). And the most appropriate stance is wise, compassionate stewardship. These are the perspectives and actions that are needed in the world, and the living systems view is (at the very least) a powerful way to get there.

Also, the living systems view appears to be the most comprehensive lens we currently have. It is expansive enough to hold many other perspectives: for example, living systems have mechanistic characteristics, as well as network properties; they offer models of competition and war, as well as collaboration and altruism. In these ways, the living systems view reveals more of reality and offers up more effective – and wiser – ways forward than the alternative lenses I'm aware of.

And still, it's not quite accurate to say it's a one-size-fits-all prescription. The living systems lens sees each organization as both inherently unique and self-healing – meaning that the most effective solutions will be those generated by the organization itself. To that end, the living systems view comes with a vast and growing toolbox of invitational and participatory processes, such as the Art of Hosting (and the myriad techniques it comprises), OpenSpace Agility, Non-Violent Communication, Asset Based Community Development and more (any of these may be explored via a simple Google search), even as it brings forward many traditional tools and approaches. Both of these points offer considerable protection against restrictive one-size-fits-all prescriptions.

2. Organizations don't have a clear physical boundary. We're accustomed to identifying organisms by their physical borders. Our own skin gives a comforting sense of definition and delineation, for example.

Yet we know that a rain forest doesn't have a clear enclosing boundary, though it clearly is a living system, with emergent characteristics and capabilities (such as climate) that can't be found at the level of any individual component or species. The same is true of ant colonies, bee hives, coral reefs... and organizations.

And anyway, how sure are we that the skin is the beginning and end of the human organism – or any other organism, for that matter? In every way, we are an inseparable function of our environment. If you look deeply enough, the dividing line between an organism and its surrounding environment becomes more and more blurry. And a strongly delineated physical boundary becomes less and less important in defining a living system.

At the same time, organizations *do* have a certain boundedness. Organizational purpose acts as a magnet, drawing otherwise divergent people together and creating convergent wholeness from their aligned actions. I imagine a conceptual field around them, with their core purpose at the center, giving a clear sense that "we are this (within the field – for example, 'We are a weight loss clinic'), and we are not that (everything outside the field – 'We are not a hair salon')." The imagined enclosing boundary of that field then becomes the organization's relational surface, the conceptual equivalent of our skin, where we interact with customers and community.

3. Organizations are socially constructed. The objection here is that organizations don't really exist in their own right, as a tree or a whale does. They exist only if and as we imagine them into being.

There is truth in that. And at the same time, they still follow the basic patterns of living systems. And so I don't find this to be an important distinction. An organization acts like a living system. We can nurture it effectively using the same principles we do for living systems. Therefore, it seems reasonable to consider each organization as a living system, even if a socially constructed one.

There's also something deeper here. Even the social aspects of the human species are part of "life." Ants communicate and collaborate to create the emergent level of life that is a colony. Trees and fungi actively collaborate to nourish and strengthen a living forest. The fact that we participate willfully (if unwittingly and often counter-productively) in life's collaborative and creative processes doesn't make the results any less "alive."

As a species and as organizational leaders in particular, our opportunity – and pressing need – is to participate consciously, intentionally and in harmony with life's processes, channeling our willful collective action toward the conditions life needs to thrive. Indeed, the circumstances are so clearly calling out to us and the evidence so compelling that I'm surprised and puzzled that there is still a debate going on. It's not as if there's an alternative perspective that's elegantly and efficiently getting us where we want to go.

3.3

Story #1: *Espace pour la vie*

THE BACKGROUND: ORIGINALLY called the Montreal Nature Museums, this organization consists of four institutions: the Botanical Gardens, the Insectarium, the Planetarium and the Biodome (several ecosystems recreated under one roof). Each is owned by the City of Montreal, which several years ago merged them administratively and then hired one director to oversee them all. The director's mandate was to create cohesion among the four and to create one powerful brand that would add significantly to Montreal's global reputation.

The challenge: Across all four institutions, passion and commitment were high among employees. However, the infrastructure was heavy and bureaucratic, and employees were weary from lack of resources. The museums were well-loved by citizens and visitors, but generally not enough to inspire regular visits. Worse than this, their message was not powerful enough to incite more environmentally responsible behavior – the ultimate goal of their efforts. Also, despite cost savings, the staff at the four museums were not pleased with being merged; they perceived themselves as fundamentally distinct, with different scientific disciplines, histories and sizes. They were hopeful about the change the visionary, charismatic new director represented. But as scientists and educators, they were also nervous; he came from the world of the arts and spoke quite a different language. Finally, they were skeptical about branding in general; they feared they would be portrayed inauthentically and that science and education would lose prominence.

The Response: Museum directors started by putting out an invitation to all 450 people from the four institutions for a day-long exploration, asking essentially: "What is the one conversation we all want to have with the world?"

Leading up to the event, the directors issued a call for "Ambassadors" within the institutions – people who were interested in supporting the project logistically, getting a behind-the-scenes understanding of it, and sharing what they knew with others in the organization. Seventy-five people came to the first meeting of the Ambassadors. Though many were more skeptical than supportive, the interest was encouraging. In addition, comment boxes were placed prominently around, with a clear invitation to staff to share their visions, hopes and fears. A flood of detailed comments flowed in.

Those comments and input from the Ambassadors then helped shape the all-day gathering. Through a series of lively, guided conversations, the event helped museum staff to articulate what it would look like when all the necessary "fertile conditions" for thrivability were in place.

The outcome was a draft manifesto that was refined first with the help of Ambassadors and then with all employees through conversations with their managers. In these discussions, one point in particular stood out. The draft version made reference to "life," and in conversations with museum directors, there was some discomfort with this. The preference was to use the word "nature," which seemed more scientific, objective and tangible, whereas "life" had the risk of being amorphous, subjective and possibly spiritual. The manifesto was completed with reference only to "nature."

A second all-employee, all-day gathering was held to affirm the manifesto and to identify next steps and "vital signs" indicating progress. Key figures from the city and the scientific community were invited to express their support. In one memorable moment, a blue-collar, union employee stood up to declare, "These are our words. They didn't come from [one high-level official]. They came from us. This is our manifesto. And that means we have to do it!"

As the search for a new all-encompassing name for the Montreal Nature Museums then got underway, discussion continued over use of the term "life." In particular, the director questioned whether it was possible to inspire meaningful change in visitor behavior through references only to nature as something "out there," surrounding us, and not to life, which is also within each of us. There was also concern over losing the individual identity of each institution. In the end, each institution maintained its original identity, and together, they became *Espace pour la vie* – the Space for Life. The new name was not only a brand to them; it was the beginning of a movement, the one conversation they all wanted to have with the world.

[As an aside, the new name also offered a convenient way of explaining the concept of "thrivability" – a word that is impossible to translate into French, but that can be understood as the intention and practice of crafting an organization as a "space for life."]

Organizational structure was then reshaped into three pillars: (divergent) People & Culture, (convergent) Visitor Engagement, and (supportive, connective) Infrastructure. This was a significant change from the previous structure, in which Human Resources was buried within Finance & Administration. There was also a broadly participatory exploration of new governance structures, in which many suggestions by employees were implemented.

Internal communication blossomed. With a compelling shared identity, there was now a willingness to open budgets to each other and to decide collaboratively how resources would be allocated (an astonishing shift, actually). For the first time, cross-organizational projects were initiated. Resident artists were introduced without specific mandate beyond offering inspiration. Whereas meetings had previously been stiff, slow and with limited impact, they now became vibrant and alive, particularly where the conversation remained focused on shared intention. Ideas flowed from inspiration to implementation almost faster than people could keep up with them.

Externally, engagement also grew. Citizens were invited into a regular (still ongoing) series of workshops to help shape the visitor experience. Museum exhibits began a steady overhaul, becoming more interactive and immersive and connecting more with the power of narrative and imagination. New projects extended into the community and, indeed, across the planet.

Though for nine years, the museums had struggled – and failed – to raise enough money to renovate the outdated Planetarium, they were now able to attract enough attention and funds to build a completely new, LEED Platinum building, with spectacular new exhibits. In fact, the power of their vision enabled them to raise $190 million, allowing them to create several other important projects, as well.

In all, the process of aligning with life's patterns has moved this organization toward being a powerful *living* movement, both inside and out.

3.4

The Trifocal Lens*

So, what changes – and what becomes possible – when we acknowledge our organizations as living systems and we enter into the practice of thrivability?

The answer is: it depends.

The possibilities the living systems patterns hold depend on the lens we use to see them.

As I mentioned at the beginning of the book, the living systems view has gained significant traction over the past two decades. And yet what I have observed is that not every organization or community has enjoyed equal benefit from it. Most achieve only modest improvements to their culture and operations, leaving plenty of opportunity on the table. But a small number cultivate something vibrantly generative – and even *regenerative* – creating unimagined benefits, so that:

---

* Some portions of this chapter originally appeared in a Huffington Post article entitled, "What You See Is What You Get: The Full Promise of the Living Systems Lens," published on February 25, 2015. Other portions appeared in a paper, co-authored with Michael Jones, called, "Living Systems Theory and the Practice of Stewarding Change," within the June 2015 issue of the journal, *Spanda*.

- **Workers and customers** experience more aliveness, health, joy, justice, learning, self-expression and self-awareness;
- The **community** discovers more connectedness, creativity, resilience and self-reliance;
- The **organization** achieves its intended purpose creatively, gracefully and resiliently, while attracting and cultivating necessary resources;
- The **biosphere** is supported in its ability to be healthy and regenerative over time.

What makes the difference between generic and generative?

Certainly, there must be many factors at play. But here is a simple yet potent metaphor for what I've noticed: if the living systems lens were actually a pair of glasses, it would be trifocals, offering three distinct views. And what you do with it – what that perspective changes and makes possible – depends on which of the three parts of the lens you look through. All three are needed. But only one leads us the full distance to thriving. Only one calls forth Daniel Bernoulli's principle of lift, engaging the human spirit and forging a transcendent path ahead.

The first lens is **instrumental and transactional** – the lens of the hands. Focused on matters closest at hand, it looks for best practices, proven solutions and tactical adjustments. This view recognizes that, like a map or a tool, the living systems patterns have direct operational value. As my colleague Michael Jones suggests, it poses the question, "How can we do things differently?"

In my own client work, this has included interviewing employees and customers (now that their divergent voices clearly matter), changing a company name and logo (to convey the genuine care that united the people within it), and improving retail décor (to make the space of infrastructure and relationship not only functional, but nourishing to living people).

Actions guided by this lens bring useful results. But ultimately, the value is limited. In general, a tool has incremental impact at best, particularly when it seeks to introduce or improve existing solutions.

The second of the three lenses is **intellectual** – the lens of the head. With a slightly broader view, this lens suggests new vocabulary (*network, ecosystem, self-organization, emergence*), and it reveals new strategies, asking, "How can we *do different things*?" Here, my work has included introducing the practices and mindsets of applied improvisation (to embrace and support emergence and collective intelligence) and reshaping governance structures (to engage more of the ecosystem in decision-making and to align with life's organizing patterns).

Actions guided by this lens have a more dramatic impact. But they still don't fundamentally shift the nature of the organization from generic to generative. They still don't fully create the conditions for thrivability.

Only the third lens – the lens of the heart – is fully **transformative**. The question becomes, "How can we *see* differently?" And **here, we discover the most far-reaching – and profound – implications of the living systems lens, as we truly begin to perceive the aliveness in our organizations, our communities and ourselves.** This is the lens that sees radical, transformational potential within the patterns, tapping into Bernoulli's principle of lift to transcend existing laws and limitations, and discovering a depth of value and implication that isn't evident from the surface of the four patterns.

This third lens draws our attention to the aspects of our lives that exist alongside and apart from reason – things like love, beauty, inspiration, meaning and purpose – and reveals them as different but equally valid expressions of what is true and valuable. What is most wounded in our world is our connection to this dimension of life. With the Era of Divergence and the rise of the industrial economy, we created a world out of balance. Scientific reason rose to dominance and our subjective experience fell into disrepute. In organizations, for example, our visions and plans became dry and lifeless, unaccompanied by the stirring story of who we are, what we stand for, what is our shared quest and why it matters. Similarly, our communities lost coherence and character, serving as nothing more than barren backdrops for impersonal transactions. With the loss of the meaning-filled dimension of our lives, we no longer had access to **gratitude and awe at the mystery of life within and around us**. We were no longer held and inspired onward by **a story of wholeness and wonder.**

In embracing the living systems lens, then, our work is not only to offer new tools or to enable intellectual awareness and agility. It is also to invite an expanded set of beliefs: belief that there is vibrant aliveness and creativity within and around us (this alone is to be savored and celebrated!); that each organization and community can (and must) shape and live into an unfolding epic narrative; and that thriving *is* possible and we are worthy of it.

Julian Giacomelli, CEO of raw, vegan, organic food services company Crudessence, commented on these beliefs in the context of his company:

[Thrivability represents] the real belief that what we are doing here is actively helping us create the world we want to live in, so that all the activities in this company aren't just interesting or good, but vital to the well-being and ongoing creation of a world that makes much more sense than what we see.[96]

It was this belief that led the company to adopt the tagline "Servir la vie" – "Serving life" – referring both to the fact that they are serving their customers "life" in the form of raw, living food, and also to their commitment to be in service of life in everything they do.

With such expanded beliefs, we open up to new conversations, new priorities, new possibilities, new relationships, new agreements, new actions, new business models, new architecture, new governance – all more fully aligned with life. We step together into wise, compassionate and meaningful engagement with life, wherever we find it – and we find it everywhere.

With this lens firmly in hand (or perhaps I should say, "in heart"), we can then connect back with our head and hands in new ways, enabling truly substantive regeneration, not only of ourselves, but of our world.

In these ways, "thrivability looks like people working together, bringing their best, contributing to a project or a plan," says Julie Bourbonnais former Assistant Director of Space for Life, Canada's largest complex of nature museums. "It looks like people meeting some really important objective."[97]

It looks like "an organization where people are first of all happy to come in, where they find meaning in what they do," adds Enspiral's Seb Paquet, "where they are in their own learning stance, and where they are taking care of each other. The organization is attending to people's needs in a responsible fashion." More than that, "There is a kind of radiance or glow around a thrivable organization that people sense when they come in contact with its people or products."[98]

For Sophie Derevianko, internal organizational development consultant at a major hydro-electric company, thrivability represents "a possibility to really tap into that raw energy that we all have inside us, and to stay connected to that raw energy as much as possible, as often as possible, and to awaken the passion within us through that energy to do good in the world."[99]

In fact, beyond "doing good" in response to the urgent need for transformation of our ailing world, the third lens reveals the glorious *opportunity* for transformation. It shows us that **the reason we do most anything is *to be transformed* – to become more fully alive and to contribute to more aliveness around ourselves.** Every interaction is an opportunity to be transformed. This is life's fundamental urge. Anything less is simply transactional, falling short of fulfilling life's true yearning.

This perspective is evident in the "transformational experience" Apple seeks to offer within their stores. "In 2001, when Steve Jobs and Ron Johnson first decided to open a store to sell Apple products, they didn't start with a vision to sell stuff," explains Carmine Gallo, author of *The Apple Experience.* "They decided the vision behind the Apple Store would be to enrich lives."[100]

A similar approach is also evident at Zenith Cleaners, where "cleaning as practice" is seen as an opportunity for transformation of the space being cleaned, but also of client, cleaner and society. This, in turn, is leading to transformative opportunities for Zenith itself. Says CEO Tolu Ilesanmi:

> By allowing the individuals to thrive and allowing thrivability within the organization, it's leading to a whole world of opportunities [for Zenith]. And so cleaning is contributing to education. Cleaning is contributing to organizational development. It expands what is possible. Because we are contributing on a higher level as an organization, it leads to a whole world of possibilities, and that's what's happening for us as an organization.[101]

Language school CLC Montreal has a similar philosophy, viewing language instruction as a means to enable human connection and therefore individual and societal transformation. On their website, for example, this is how they describe "what they care about most":

> We want many things from our work together: happy and successful students, a feeling of excellence and accomplishment, a thriving business, personal growth and recognition, a strong sense of community.

> But at the deepest level, we want to contribute to a world in which there is more joy, more understanding, more love. And to us, learning a language is a powerful way to do this:

> - We create a space and an experience in which people can feel joy, understanding and love.
> - And then, with greater ability to connect with others through language, our students leave us well-equipped to create even more joy, understanding and love in the world.

> These are the things we care about most.[102]

These are rare examples, but they don't have to be. Says Zenith's Ilesanmi:

It's our natural state to be thrivable. It's our natural state to be fully engaged at every level of our being. [Thrivability is] not something we use. It's what we are. It's how we are supposed to be. And it's why when there's thrivability in an organization, everything comes alive.... It affects every aspect of the organization. It affects the relationships internally, externally. It affects sales. Because you want to move toward this organization. There's something exciting, joyful, playful. And you want to participate. It's more than useful. I see it as our true state as human beings, to be thrivable, to be fully alive.[103]

Through these examples, we see that only by looking through all three facets of the living systems lens do we open ourselves to the full possibility of thriving. Only in this way is our practice of stewardship fully enlivened. Only here do we discover a pathway into an Age of Thrivability.

3.5

Story #2: Zenith Cleaners

[Written by Tolu Ilesanmi, Cleaner and CEO of Zenith Cleaners, a successful Montreal-based business offering commercial and residential cleaning services. You can learn more about Zenith at www.zenithcleaners.com.]

THERE IS PERHAPS no service or job that seems more mundane and more lacking in promise than cleaning. The work of a cleaner tends to be transactional, impersonal, perpetuating a sense of shame and stigma. I came into it from business school because I loved its simplicity in comparison with complicated b-school theories and models of change. But I had to face the fact that cleaning is considered by most to be a dead-end job or at best a temporary stepping stone.

And yet I was drawn to the side of cleaning that we as a society were not engaging with – the idea of cleaning as a practice and a metaphor. My sense was that the business of cleaning was preventing cleaning from fulfilling its potential as a transformative practice that affects both object and subject, both cleaner and the thing being cleaned, both the agent of change and the object of change.

In fact, as I and the people I am very privileged to attract into cleaning for the love of it persisted in bearing witness to this other side of cleaning, we could not escape the simplicity and the profundity of what we were working and playing with. This led us to articulate what we saw as the essence of cleaning:

"Cleaning is the process of removing dirt from any space, surface, object or subject thereby revealing beauty, potential, truth and sacredness."

At the root of this understanding is stewardship, bringing care, attention and presence to a space, removing obstructions to the flow of life energy, creating conditions for both objects and subjects to thrive. When we go into a space to clean, we do not own the space or anything there. Our task is simply to remove dirt and render the space beautiful, to restore wholeness and return it to its essence. In a sense, we go in to care and to heal, and then we leave when our task is done. And then, after we clean, people can do whatever it is they want and are capable of doing in the space - we have freed both space and potential, for a time.

Through cleaning, we came to understand that while stewardship has elements of control – shifting things around, moving dirt from where it blocks potential and obstructs beauty to where it nourishes – it is essentially creating or allowing the conditions for life to thrive, for something bigger, something epic to emerge, like a gardener does by weeding a garden. At Zenith, cleaning became no longer just a service we offer, but our practice.

This understanding seemed to unshackle cleaning, freeing it to do what it has always wanted to do – to transform not only the tangible, but the intangible. Indeed, it is hard not to see how this principle applies not only to physical spaces or to the act of cleaning, but also to leadership and everything on the planet we engage with. Perhaps we are here, wherever here is – this home, this project, this organization, this community, this country, this planet, this life – to reveal beauty, restore wholeness, return tangible or intangible things to essence, to truth and to sacredness and then to leave when our task is done.

Recognizing this emboldened me to embrace the identity of "the Cleaner," regardless of the stigma attached to it. The absurdity of being ashamed of something whose purpose is unveiling beauty became crystal clear, the way one must appreciate the dirtiness of a space in order to clean it. Being a Cleaner in a world in dire need of transformation becomes a thing to celebrate and not a thing to be ashamed of.

For clients, our approach to cleaning not only ensures them great service, it exposes them to a new perspective that transforms their relationship to cleaners, cleaning and their work. What is more, it earns us their fierce loyalty.

For employees, we've created a space where they feel nourished and fully alive for however long they are with us. During that time, they are often inspired to come up with and implement new ideas. In what we call "Cleaning Storms," for example, we partner with local community organizations to help people who would love a clean space, but have no time to clean or no money to hire cleaners. In two hours, a group of cleaners totally transforms their home for free and for fun.

For our business, an expansive view of cleaning has broadened our offerings, opened new doors and created new opportunities outside the scope of a traditional cleaning service. For instance, in addition to commercial and residential cleaning services, we now offer "Cleaning as Practice" experiences to organizations and individuals. After all, why should cleaning, with all its potency, simplicity and accessibility apply only to school hallways and not apply to how and what we learn and teach? Through these experiences, we invite people to be cleaners for a time and then to reflect on their experience. Among the many benefits and insights that are revealed, the act of cleaning together increases one's sense of belonging and evokes a sense of ownership that has more to do with the privilege of service and stewardship than possessiveness or control. The result is that beauty, truth and sacredness are revealed for people, organizations and even industries. Now, when we consider cleaning a bank, we are of course thinking of cleaning the banking hall and washrooms, but also of participating in returning banking to its essence, free of corruption or dirtiness, where transactions are subordinate to human relationships.

Importantly, we continuously apply this same cleaning lens to Zenith itself – to our culture, our operations, our internal and external relationships and our finances.

The beauty of cleaning is that it must happen again and again. This fact makes our work very dynamic, always getting richer, because we are not just cleaning; we are being cleaned.

3.6

THE CALL TO STEWARDSHIP

THERE IS A certain amount of *reverence* that comes when you see something – really see it – as alive. When you understand that it has a life of its own. That it exists for its own ends. That it has potential that can't fully be known and that may or may not be completely realized, depending on countless influences and interactions. There is mystery and magic in something that is alive.

For a direct and simple experience of this kind of reverence, find the point on your neck where your pulse is strongest. Take a moment to feel the rhythm, silently breathing in a sense of wonder at the life flowing through you, animating you, powering you all these years, creating you, healing you, propelling you for a time. You are alive. That is something to marvel at and be grateful for. Your aliveness is something worthy of profound reverence.

With reverence comes an invitation to care. We are wired with a sense of care – care for ourselves and those close to us, certainly, but also a broader compassion for all living things, with an inherent sense of kinship and responsibility - even the most hardened among us.

And when reverence and responsibility are ignited together within us, the result is a personal call to stewardship.

Isn't this what we crave, really? To see the world with wonder, reverence and awe? And to feel called to care and be of service?

Here, service is not the same as servitude (which is why I find the phrase "servant leader" less compelling than "steward"). My parenting is service, both to my children and to the society they will serve in turn. I don't own or control my children. With love and reverence and a great deal of trust in life, I accompany and support them – sometimes actively, sometimes less so – providing the fertile conditions for them to thrive and for them to contribute to thriving in the world. Yet I am not their servant. I am a steward of my children's lives. And in the same spirit, we can be stewards of our organizations, our communities and the Earth.

Such stewardship is not a discrete set of competencies that can be trained and certified. It is not a "to do" list. Instead, it is an ongoing personal practice, like a martial arts or spiritual practice, ever unfolding as the context changes, as the living system you are cultivating unfolds, and as *you* grow and evolve through the process. It is a craft developed over time through experience, imitation and intuition. It is the lifelong journey of growing into wisdom, compassion and the ability to sense what is needed and to respond with effective action.

A fellow champion of living systems perspectives recently told me he doesn't use the word stewardship in his work because "it implies that we know better" – better than life, as I understood his sentiment. Instead he uses the word "gardening." But to me, gardening can too easily be dismissed as an idle hobby. Stewardship, on the other hand, is more clearly a calling. And sometimes stewardship *does* call for wise action, *precisely* because we know better – not better *than* life, but better *with* life. Better *on behalf of* life.

There are rich layers to the idea of a "calling," as I discovered recently when I co-hosted a week-long retreat on a five-acre wooded island north of Toronto. We were there to explore the deeper role of "place" for our communities, our work, and ourselves. It was a beautiful experience with many profound insights. And most of all, it felt like a nourishing taste of what is possible in community.

As we arrived, we explored the island, getting to know its many features, some of them crafted by human hands, much of it wild. Stopping at points along the way, we shared our stories with each other, weaving ourselves into this place.

On one of the following days, we each went to the part of the island that *called* to us, where we felt the strongest sense of home. There, we reflected and wrote in our journals, asking: "What does 'home' mean to me, and how do I get there?"

A cheerfully clanging bell signaled that it was time to come back together, and I was surprised to notice the intense joy I felt at the sound – at being *called* back into belonging. Already, these were people I had come to love. Perhaps more precisely, I had come to love who and how we all were together.

As we gathered again, we moved into a common project, taking on a meaningful task together. (In fact, we cleaned our space together, led by Tolu Ilesanmi of Zenith Cleaners.) And we talked about what it means to share a *calling* – to feel called to work toward the same goal.

What I later learned is that the origins of the word "calling" are the same as the word "beauty," which was also strongly present throughout our experience on the island. As Michael Jones relates: "The word beauty itself is closely related to both calling and compassion. As such, beauty lies at the root of what it means to be truly compassionate and truly alive. It is our *call* to life. To be regenerative is to return the world to beauty."[104]

At the end of our time together, I was fascinated to notice the different ways we had experienced the concept of a "call" – one personal and divergent; one relational; one rooted in collective, convergent action; and one ethereal and inspiring, a call to life itself. What we found was that when all of these aspects were present and coherent with each other, our work felt joyful, effective, inspired and transformative. The feeling was one of flow and celebration – of thrivability. We were experiencing the full living systems pattern, with place playing a strong supporting role. And we each felt strongly called into stewardship of that pattern.

As I reflect on these different experiences of being called, my sense is that the "responsibility" within stewardship of our human communities is most of all "response-ability." It is a response to each of those four calls:

(1) to an inner call to come home to ourselves, to our bodies and to the places and stories that shape us;

(2) to our pining for rich belonging and a sense of sacredness in our relationships with the human and more-than-human world;

(3) to a calling or purpose that propels us into transformative, generative action together;

(4) and to the call to life that our yearning for beauty and celebration carries within it.

In our organizations and communities, then, **stewardship is less a role or a title and more a commitment to tend to each of these fertile conditions, offered from a stance of reverence for the life in each of us and between us, as well as for the transcendent potential that we may express together.** In this way, what we are stewarding is the fullness of a system's ongoing ability to thrive – its thrivability.

There is paradox woven into this view of stewardship – in reverence for something beyond our full control or comprehension, but commitment to care for it nonetheless. Similarly, there is paradox in stewardship's call at times to trust life's process of emergence, passively "holding space," while at other times actively intervening and even on occasion making way for death. Stewardship demands both patient detachment and fierce determination. "A most worthy dance," as a friend once said.

What, then, of management and leadership? Are these approaches obsolete?

The answer lies in our familiar set of patterns.

MANAGEMENT CONTROLS

Management continues to be appropriate for the useful, surface-level busyness of the day-to-day, with its focus on controlling the parts, rather than the system as a whole, through tactics, action plans, performance goals, and expert-driven solutions in a push to achieve certain, generally known, outcomes.

Leadership Guides

As we shift our focus from efficiency of parts to effectiveness of interactions, leadership becomes the stance of choice. Where relationship and infrastructure are the primary leverage points, leadership offers guidance (rather than control) through strategies, structures and processes. The leader shapes human dynamics through influence and incentives, as well as through shared values and principles. While management helps us get to known, predictable outcomes, leadership helps us get to what fellow thrivability champion Jean Russell calls "guessable outcomes."* When a team works on new product design, for example, we can guess what the outcome will be, but we can't really know with certainty. The situation is simply too complex to predict. But it can be *guided* with effective leadership.

Stewardship Nurtures

While intervening around strategies, structures and relationships can bring about significant results, if we seek adaptability and regenerativity – if our aim is to grow the capacity of the system – then we shift from managing the parts and leading for effectiveness to stewarding the health of the whole, in all its potential. Here, control and guidance are replaced by encouragement and invitation, with continuous iteration and attention to emergent patterns of "what wants to happen." The goal is not to control, but to create the fertile conditions for something new and unknowable to emerge. The intention is to nurture the system's intrinsic and ongoing capacity for learning, innovation, self-organization and, ultimately, thriving.

---

* Jean Russell writes about these three approaches – which she describes as Control, Guide and Nurture – in a very insightful model called the Action Spectrum. I've drawn significantly on that model here. This and more of her writing can be found at www.thrivable.net, as well as in her book, *Thrivability: Breaking Through to a World That Works*.

When a community has identified the need for revitalization, for example, the traditional approach would be to create a strategic plan behind closed doors, plotting the course with precision and carefully controlling the flow of resources. Instead, with faith in the life that exists throughout the community, a process of invitation and encouragement can be set into motion, connecting people to each other and to their unspoken dreams for themselves and for their shared experience of community... revealing hidden gifts and releasing pent-up energy... and cultivating the community's inherent capability to thrive.

Though most every organization has need of management and leadership, **only the call of stewardship guides us toward continuous generativity – toward cultivating fertile ground and manifesting new possibilities for the future.**

To enable the system to take on a life of its own and to help it become truly, gloriously generative, the challenge of stewardship is to navigate a thoughtful mix of control, guidance and nurturing; to tend to both individual and collective; and to support the system's wisdom, learning and enrichment, as well as its accomplishment of tasks and milestones. Along the way, the wise steward's questions include: What would bring the most life to this situation? What is the wisdom that is needed now? What seems to want to come to life here? How can I serve this unfolding, either by disturbing things, by planting a seed, by cultivating a freshly sprouted initiative, or by compassionately hospicing something that needs to die?

Throughout, stewardship embraces uncertainty and invites learning, innovation and play. It recognizes emergent collective wisdom, developing individual and shared disciplines to listen for the voice of the whole even as it honors the needs of the parts. Stewardship requires thoughtful crafting of structures and systems. It necessarily takes a holistic view – which in organizations means linking purpose with passion, brand with culture, and worker with customer and community. And it acknowledges that place, art and nature have a vital role to play in every sphere of our lives.

3.7

STORY #3: CLC MONTREAL

[Written by AJ Javier, founder and General Director at CLC. You can learn more about this thriving Montreal-based language school at www.clcmontreal.com.]

THE THREE LETTERS of our school's name stand for *Culture & Language Connections*. As evocative as those three words are, there is more to us than even they reveal.

In fact, in our marketing, we say that CLC feels like home, no matter where you're from. And it's true.

If you think about it, that's kind of surprising. Learning a new language always changes you – you can't help but grow, as you learn new words and sounds... as you come to understand a different culture... and as you build new relationships with people from other parts of the world. In our space, people grow and change, always in unexpected ways.

So how is it that, in the middle of all this newness and change, people find a deep sense of belonging, as if they've arrived home, at last? How can it be that they discover themselves along the way?

To be honest, we're not quite sure ourselves. There's something a little like alchemy in the culture that has been woven into this space. Whatever it is, we treasure it.

Since its founding in 2009, CLC has grown into a dynamic, successful language school and a vibrant community – quite a remarkable accomplishment, considering the intense competition we face.

The time my wife and I spent living and teaching in Japan has greatly influenced much of what CLC is today. The idea to open a school came only after returning to Canada and connecting the dots – a space that blended the best educational practices of the West with the systems approach of the Japanese. The school would lie at the intersection of culture, language and connections.

Beyond these surface concepts, however, the seeds for the school's emergence lay even deeper – in people's yearning to find meaning in their lives. My intention was not to exploit an opportunity *per se*, but to fill an empty space in people's hearts... to bring people together... to help them thrive. Indeed, the primary mission has always been to help people feel more fully alive. The school simply provides a familiar framework people recognize and feel comfortable to enter.

Fueled by this vision and the energy that comes with starting a new business, the first year flew by in a blur. But as this honeymoon period gave way to the reality of ongoing operations, we struggled and searched for a way forward. Without any formal business education or experience, we were guided by instinct and the underlying mission we had set out for the school. But this instinct seemed to go against much of the conventional wisdom about how a business is "supposed" to be run, and doubts began to arise. Then we discovered the concept of thrivability, which aligned remarkably well with our thinking. At last, we had an established model to compare ourselves to, to use as a sounding board and to reflect upon.

In fact, we had always recognized CLC as a very organic organization. For example, we rarely refer to it as a "school" or "organization" or "business." We talk about it as "the space," meaning: the sum of all the life, experiences, contributions and growth of everyone who enters it. With this perspective, our first inclination was to take a cue from nature... to let the space grow "wild" and find its own path. But we eventually realized a better metaphor would be that of a garden, protected and nurtured by loving hands. In this way, thrivability has become an invaluable lens to invite everyone who enters the community to become a steward, contributing to its growth and growing personally in the process. To us, engaging with CLC should be a transformative experience. This is the synergy that drives the success of the space.

With inspiration from living systems principles, we have discerned four pillars that foster success within our space. The first pillar is the discovery and support of talent and the celebration of the authentic self. People are studying languages here, but it is usually just a skill necessary to move forward on a greater front... to fulfill dreams. The pursuit of interests and ultimately self-actualization is the engine that propels people. This focus creates an almost electric environment that offers people the freedom to change.

The second pillar is cultivation of community. At a basic level, language needs to be shared. It does not reside in a textbook or as something learned and then stored away; it is something that is practiced and used. Language lives in the space between people – in other words, in community. Within our space, community serves as the witness that celebrates and encourages the growth of the individual learner. This builds the trust that is necessary for people to be open and willing to accept feedback. People accept themselves and accept the diversity of the community. As barriers fall, the ability to learn grows, and bonds deepen. By the time people leave the school, they have found a second home and often cry in parting. These are tears of celebration and recognition that, on the path of their lives, they have come across a special place – and a special community – that will live within them always.

The third pillar is continuous improvement of our offering and operations. This has enabled us to craft an uncommonly effective teaching methodology, and it generates an attitude and atmosphere of dynamism and possibility.

The final pillar is faith. We simply believe that good comes to people who do good.

In all of these ways, CLC doesn't just teach languages; it helps people compose the song of their lives and sing it.

3.8

Embodying All the Patterns

As we explore the concept of thrivability and the practice of stewardship, it becomes clear that what we are really talking about is embodying all four of the living systems patterns in our work together. And that can be challenging to grasp. For example, what does it mean to act like a divergent part? Or a self-integrating property?

We may find helpful support for this in an unexpected place. I was fascinated to learn that the four living systems patterns are mirrored again in a set of archetypes discovered originally by psychologist Carl Jung and developed further and popularized in the 1990s by several authors (most notably Robert L. Moore and Douglas Gillette).[105] According to Jung, these archetypal images are patterns of thought and behavior present in all cultures and all people across all of human history. Importantly, they do not represent personality types or personal roles. They are timeless "energies" that each of us is capable of bringing forth in different circumstances, though we may generally have more comfort with one than with the others. As with the living systems patterns, each of the archetypes is needed in any project team that hopes to generate new possibilities. Moreover, I find that they help unlock the deeper implications of the patterns, describing, in a way, how we *live* the patterns together.

The first archetype is the **Warrior**. It is the push for individual expression – for bringing forth our unique gifts, talents and inner truth – and it carries the energy of

divergence. Decisive and action-oriented, it is the source of our fierceness, conviction and loyalty. It represents rationality and discipline and is the realm of skill and technology. Warrior energy is present when we are responsive, resourceful and prepared. Without reassurance that its divergence is protected, the Warrior resists the call of the other archetypes. And as much as it is the energy of divergence, fully developed Warrior energy is channeled in service of a cause larger than ourselves, guided by overarching ideals and principles.

The second archetypal image is the **Magician** (sometimes called the Weaver). As the energy of **relationship**, pattern and process, this is the alchemist of lore who weaves together unrelated things to create the conditions for emergent possibility. This archetype "sees the world from many different angles," explains Michael Jones, "invit[ing] new possibilities in a spirit of generosity, detachment, perspective and novelty." This is where we find specialized knowledge and an advisor's ability to interpret complex situations, making them appear simple. We see the Magician present in skilful meeting facilitation or in one who connects ideas and people in the interest of insight, learning and innovation. It is present in the design of new organizing structures. And it is the realm of rites of passage and other meaningful patterns of life.

The third archetype is the **Sovereign** (sometimes called the King), representing **wholeness**, order, coherence, shared vision and purpose. This is not about any one person *being* the sovereign. It is about the urge to gather around a compelling cause – to be part of an unfolding heroic narrative. This archetype calls for invitation, rather than persuasion or coercion, and for discernment – "we are this, together, and not that." It inspires a culture of generosity and recognition of gifts, a vital component of generativity.* In these ways, Sovereign energy is associated with healing through making whole, as well as with creativity, fertility and leaving a lasting legacy. If you find yourself asking how the organization is walking its talk or imagining a bold vision of what is possible, you are expressing Sovereign energy.

---

* Organizational scholar CV Harquail writes about the connection between generosity and generativity in her insightful article: From Generativity to Generosity: What's at the core of these new business practices? This and more of her writing can be found at www.authenticorganizations.com.

The fourth and final archetype is the **Enchanter** (sometimes called the Lover), bringing in the **animating and self-integrating spark of life** through the energy of renewal, festival and transformative celebration. The root of the word "enchanter" means to sing into being. This energy is accessed through beauty, art, music, nature, play, dance and inspiration – the dominion of the Muses. Embodying the realm of emotion and sensuality, the presence of this energy makes us feel fully alive and filled with passion. In these ways, the Enchanter "connects us to the transcendent," as Michael Jones puts it.

This energy can be strongly present in a person and, to some degree, it can be designed into a moment; but in my experience, it can also burst through when the other three energies are present – when each person is actively able to bring forward the best of themselves, when patterns of interaction are free-flowing and healthy, and when everyone is working together toward a meaningful shared purpose. Life flows through everyone in a river's rush and work feels like play, like celebration, like something sacred, even.

As we acknowledge the potency of Jung's archetypes, the work of stewardship can be seen as ensuring that all four of these energies are present in an appropriate mix and brought forth at useful times within a project or organization.

Practically speaking, thinking in terms of these archetypes can help us understand why people value different things within a project and why not everyone can always understand what we value. If I'm pushing for action while another member of the team wants to leave time for insight to emerge from a collective process, we can acknowledge that I'm likely operating from valuable Warrior energy and the other person is probably bringing useful Magician energy. We can rise above personalities and personal conflict, recognizing the validity and importance of each type of energy, asking which one is most needed at this moment and exploring whether there are ways to integrate both into the effort.

In the early-stages of a project I was involved in recently, this was played out with striking clarity. Four of us were considering whether to collaborate on a multi-day festival that would bring together visionary thinkers and do-ers from a very active global Facebook group. My Sovereign proposal was to orient the festival around a guiding theme: what does it mean to craft a city as a space for life? "We could even frame the flow of the experience according to the patterns of life," I offered, "guiding people through experiences of their own divergence and the divergence of their projects, then relationship with each other, then experimenting with convergence. Beauty and inspiration would be woven throughout. And we could make those patterns explicit so they could be useful and supportive to people after the festival."

"No, no, no," said my Warrior colleague. "I'm tired of meaning-making. What I want is to be in action, to prototype and to identify which new business models are working best, for example, and which land ownership structures are most appropriate."

"No, no, no," said my Magician friend. "What I think is needed is space and time to be together in emergence. Let's just see what happens when we bring all these people together physically within a thoughtfully hosted experience of deep connection, without the restriction of a guiding theme or conceptual framework."

The fourth member of our group didn't offer an opinion. Pure Enchanter that he was, he happily volunteered to bring his piano, poetry and inspiring stories, if invited.

I was fascinated at how clearly we were embodying all four of the archetypes, in turn. And I noticed how, even with awareness of this, it was difficult to come to a shared vision of how they might all be integrated – how they might enhance and not restrict each other.

In the end, my Magician friend won out and the event was a beautiful – "magical" – experience of deep connection among participants. And that has allowed a natural emergence of mutual support, collective projects and shared identity.

Our small group's struggle highlights the challenge – and the learning practice – the steward must take on. Perhaps in some cases, the patterns must be introduced gradually, rather than all at once. Often, people need enough reassuring experiences of

Warrior and Magician before they are able to trust the invitation of the Sovereign and Enchanter archetypes. And in other situations, the Sovereign invitation to wholeness may need to be refined and made more broadly resonant before it can be embraced, including ensuring it comes unfettered by any personal issues (something true for all the archetypes, in fact). These are the types of questions and choices the steward must discern.

Similarly, the steward's challenge can be made more difficult by strong cultural biases toward one or more of the archetypes, and aversion toward others. In my experience, for example, Quebec culture strongly favors the Magician and Enchanter archetypes (no wonder it is the birthplace of Cirque du Soleil!) and is generally suspicious of Sovereign energy (which may be one reason it has the lowest level of entrepreneurship in Canada). And my experience working in various parts of the United States has shown me that Warrior energy is highly valued, while the others are considered optional add-ons at best or irrelevant distractions at worst.

In many circumstances, the Sovereign seems to be a particularly wounded archetype. Rightfully so, we've become suspicious of it, associating it with cult, religion, dictators and corrupt ego-driven leaders. Often enough, our Warrior energy fears loss of individual voice. And our Magician assumes lifeless bureaucracy and excessive control.

But without the invitation into wholeness and higher purpose that the Sovereign archetype offers, we struggle to get to full generativity – to creating a whole greater than the sum of its parts. Without deference to a Sovereign story or cause, for example, Warrior and Magician easily fall into conflict. The Warrior wants to get things done, while the Magician wants to create ample space and time for connection and emergence. The Warrior favors inner truth and inspiration, whereas the Magician is suspicious of individual motives and favors collective wisdom. It becomes challenging to integrate the two.

Digging more deeply into such predispositions, it can be helpful to note that the first two archetypes (Warrior and Magician) are instrumental, lending themselves to easy validity, particularly as we come out of an era dominated by rational thought alone. The final two archetypes (Sovereign and Enchanter) have less direct connection to the action, and yet they tend to bring transformative, rather than instrumental impact. Think of the power of Steve Jobs' vision, for example, which included a rare emphasis on both heroic ambition and art and inspiration. He embodied both Sovereign and Enchanter, and those values continue to drive the success of Apple, even after his death.

In essence, this whole book is an entreaty on behalf of the transformative energies of Sovereign and Enchanter. It asks: how can we embrace a story of life and wholeness, recognizing that this can be supportive, rather than restrictive? And how can we welcome wonder, creativity and inspiration into our every experience? The sustainability and corporate social responsibility movements have been characterized by useful Warrior energy, appealing to each of us to *do things differently*. The social innovation movement has guided us in exploring new structures and methods for interacting, inviting us to *do different things*. But none of these has fully invited us to *see differently*. None has invited us into a story of healing, wholeness and inspiration. What is still needed is the transformative presence of both Sovereign and Enchanter. What is needed in the Age of Thrivability is skilful integration of all four archetypes.

3.9

Story #4: Experiencing Mariposa

Re-imagining a Mythic Story of Community

[Written by Michael Jones, long-time resident of the town of Orillia, Ontario, as well as a leadership educator, author of a series of books on reimagining leadership, and accomplished pianist with 16 albums of original piano compositions.]

As we acknowledge aliveness in our organizations and communities, we're increasingly able to draw on a broader form of knowing that some call a "mythic worldview." Author Karen Armstrong writes that in most pre-industrial cultures, "there were two recognized ways of thinking, speaking, and coming to know our world. The Greeks called them *mythos* and *logos*. Both were essential and neither was considered superior to the other. They were not in conflict, but complementary." *Logos* was the voice of reason, and timeless *mythos* the language of the imagination and our felt life together.

For too long, we have relied upon the harsh glare of the flashlight to illuminate our world and failed to realize how much it blinded us from seeing the subtle and opaque forms of the mythic world that the flickering light of the candle brings into view. To truly understand and influence a living organization or community, and to heal our collective wounds, we must bring these two ways of knowing – and seeing – back into balance.

We reconnect with the mythic dimension of life most directly through a sense of place – of being rooted in and nourished by place, of weaving our own story together with the stories of the places we belong to.

This has certainly been the case for us in Orillia, Ontario, a town that has been in the process of rekindling its mythic story.

For the past several years, I have acted as the co-chair of two community round-tables in Orillia, a rural farming and – at one time – successful industrial center 90 minutes north of the city of Toronto. Nestled on the shores of Lake Couchiching, it has long served as a gateway to the great white pine forests and near-wilderness of Central Ontario. Our task on the roundtables has been to address Orillia's downtown revitalization, economic development, cultural and event planning, infrastructure design and more. Through public conversations, individual initiatives and the support of city staff, our focus has been on what makes our community unique and how to redefine our role as citizens.

In this work, we have been accompanied – in spirit, at least – by the Canadian humorist, Stephen Leacock, who a century ago gathered together his observations and composites of the townspeople of Orillia and transported them into the much loved imaginary community of Mariposa within his book, *Sunshine Sketches of a Little Town*. Just as John Muir was an iconic figure whose work contributed to preserving and animating the wilderness ecologies and mythic origins in North America, Leacock was pivotal, in the midst of the great upheavals of war and industrial progress, in animating the longing for places that preserved our common humanity, including communities that could function on a human scale. His humorous and beguiling stories captured the imagination of readers around the world, many of whom traveled to Orillia in search of an opportunity to relive this myth for themselves.

What they found here, however, was a community still proud of its industrial past, but now in sharp economic decline. Like many other midsized communities, it was long in search of a new narrative for the future that could build upon the industrial legacy from its past. For decades, this involved living in anticipation of an industry that would adopt Orillia as its new home. But as time passed, it became apparent that the community needed not to craft a new chapter in an old story but instead to change the nature of the story itself.

It was this insight that inspired the roundtables to imagine together how the story of place as told in Leacock's Mariposa could serve as a touchstone to which many community initiatives could be measured and understood. In reimagining our own stories in this way, we took up the call to be anthropologists, uncovering the untold tales, forgotten artifacts, mysterious images and hidden meanings in order to polish and burnish them so that they might shine again and serve as the foundations of the community story.

Our desire to change the nature of our community's story also led us to explore the region's other, more ancient narrative – the indigenous story of Mnjikaning. Long before Orillia was an industrial economy, it was a gathering place – a destination for conversation amongst indigenous tribes and travelers from throughout northeastern Canada and the US. Mnjikaning means "gathering together," and for millennia many gathered here from all directions to draw nourishment and strength from the fish that were found in the clear waters.

But it was not only the fish that made this a meaningful destination for so many. It was the creative energy of the land and the hospitality of the people who made their home in that place. They were the "keepers of the fish fence," or the weirs, which are still located in The Narrows, a small channel that links two large lakes: Lake Simcoe, a deep, windswept lake to the south, and Lake Couchiching, a narrow, long, shallow winding finger lake to the north.

This land also marked the meeting place of the limestone plain and the warm, shallow pickerel lakes to the south and the deep granite and cold trout lakes of the pre-Cambrian shield to the north. To the south were mosquitoes and strawberries; to the north, blueberries and black flies. The people of Mnjikaning were unique in that they lived simultaneously in this natural creative incubator between two worlds – a "land in the middle" – where they were required to be masters of two distinct biospheres, each with its own complex ecology of fish, fauna and vegetation.

Flashing forward in time, Leacock's mythical Mariposa and the indigenous story of Mnjikaning offered our community a ray of hope, an evocative narrative not only from the past, but for the future – a recognition that in the fading of its industrial past there is a new story of place emerging in which the community may realize its potential as a place of meeting, a destination for global conversations, and an opportunity for visitors to develop their creative potential through active participation in culture, the arts, indigenous wisdom and the natural environment – experiences unique to the place itself. Underlying all of this, our vision has been to create an ethic and culture of local hospitality.

This vision led us to imagine our new public library not only as a book repository (the extent of the library board's original vision), but as a public meeting space and the physical heart of the community – a 'commons' where many with diverse interests can meet and talk.

It also led us to imagine how to fill our public spaces in a beautiful way. This has included designating a part of our downtown as an 'arts district.' It has also included seeing the downtown as a space for street closings, in order to celebrate our local culture through music and arts festivals that literally bring our streets alive.

Our belief is that the future will belong to those communities that are attuned to story, empathy, artistry, dialogue, originality and shared meaning – mythic dimensions that express their unique character and strengths. They will hold a distinct advantage over those communities who, through analysis and logic alone, tend to frame their priorities primarily in economic, technical or business terms.

3.10

MEASURING THRIVABILITY

FOR SOME REASON, it's only MBA students who ask me: how do you measure thrivability? Maybe other people assume that thrivability lies somehow beyond quantification. But the question of measurement is solidly at the heart of every self-respecting MBA program.

In fact, it's a valid question, though it might need rephrasing and reframing.

If the standard MBA refrain is, "If you can't measure it, you can't manage it," then we have to ask: What do we hope to manage within a living organization and, therefore, what do we want to measure? Who needs to do the measuring and who needs to know the results? And what about the things that lie beyond both management and measurement?

Within the mechanistic view of organizations, the goal is constant growth of output and profit. And what we want to manage (meaning: predict and control) are the resources and processes that lead to those outcomes.

What we have learned about living organizations, on the other hand, is that their goal includes far more than just growth of output and profit, and only *some* things can be predicted, controlled or managed – but that those things are still present and relevant; therefore, many of the traditional measures will continue to be useful. "What is the difference between our revenue and our expenses?" "To what extent have we reduced waste or inefficiency in our processes over time?" These are still useful questions that provide insight into the organization's health.

Health and Thriving

At the same time, quantitative measures of health only tell *part* of the story, and arguably not the most important part.

Think, for example, about what comes to mind if I ask you: "Are you healthy?" You probably scan your body, think about whether there are any diseases or injuries, or any discomfort or limitations to your physical capabilities. You might even consult a doctor for information about your blood pressure, heart rate, cholesterol level. These are quantitative, externally measurable and observable phenomena that qualify you as healthy, or not.

Similarly, any organization will find value in the equivalent "vital signs" that indicate the state of its health.

But what if I ask you if you are *thriving*?

With this question, a whole new category of scans comes into play, including those quantitative measures of health listed above *and also* qualitative dimensions like:

- The story you have about yourself and your life.
- How you feel about your relationships with other people.
- How you perceive the contribution you're making in the world.
- Your means of expressing yourself, in all your uniqueness.
- The presence of humor in your life.
- To what degree you feel a sense of progress.

- To what degree you (also) feel a sense of presence, gratitude and celebration of what is.
- How nourishing your physical surroundings are.
- Your sense of resilience in the face of change.

These are some of the aspects of your life you might assess if you wanted to measure your level of thriving. We could probably force a quantitative measure of them – "On a scale of 1 to 10, how would you rate your relationships?" for example. But fundamentally, they are subjective and qualitative.

Above, I asserted that quantitative, objective measures of health only tell part of the story, and arguably not the most important part. Here, I propose that the qualitative aspects of thriving are the missing "most important part."

But doesn't everything rest on physical health? Doesn't thriving fly out the window if you don't have basic well-being?

Maybe. But maybe not.

First, there is overwhelming scientific evidence of the power of the mind and emotions (of the subjective, in other words) to determine physical health. What this means is that you are more likely to suffer objective health issues if you are not subjectively thriving.

Conversely, some people are capable of finding great meaning in their lives even in the midst of serious health challenges, while others in perfect health die of heartbreak.[106] Taking care of the body without taking care of the spirit is not a prescription for a life well-lived.

Indeed, the characteristics of thriving naturally stir up energy, collaboration and creativity that support us in finding pathways to health. Psychiatrist and concentration camp survivor Viktor Frankl found that these qualities "strengthened the prisoner, helped him adapt, and thereby improved his chances of survival."[107]

On the other hand, the value of exclusively pursuing quantitative, objective measures of survival and health – of stoically "focusing on the basics" – has never been proven as a viable path to thriving.

Indeed, paradoxically, you may become stuck in survival mode *because* you're not attending to the factors that lead to thriving. In isolation, anxiety and depression, you can't be connected in healthy relationship. You can't see new possibilities. You can't be creative. You can't observe and participate in system dynamics. The practice of thrivability is *precisely* the path out of survival mode.

TURNING MASLOW UPSIDE-DOWN

But what about Maslow's hierarchy of needs?

Our understanding of Maslow's famous pyramid is actually upside-down: it turns out that our survival and health depend on the conditions necessary for thriving – belonging, self-actualization, meaning and self-transcendence. *Without these*, our access to other "levels" is compromised. Maslow's hierarchy is not a linear progression, nor is it actually a hierarchy. It is a collection of *dimensions* of thriving, all of which are needed.

Indeed, the primacy we have given to quantitative, objective aspects of our work and our lives has had disastrous consequences at every level.

Yet this still leaves the question of measurement: how <u>do</u> you know if you're thriving, subjectively or otherwise?

SENSING THE STORY

In our search for measures of thrivability, it may be helpful to remember that the root of the word "accounting" is the same as the French word "raconter" – to tell a story, to give an account. It's less about *counting* and more about *creating a narrative* in support of greater understanding. The question becomes: what are the cues that will give us an accurate sense of the unfolding story our organization is living out?

At the Space for Life museums, for example, they began to pay attention to the level of energy and creativity felt in meetings and what proportion of each agenda was dedicated to serving people and their passions, rather than to serving process and infrastructure. This was an important point for them, as they worked to shift from a heavily bureaucratic culture to a more nimble and creative one.

At language school CLC Montreal, founder AJ Javier shared some of the ways he assesses the level of thrivability in his organization:

- What's the level of attractiveness? ("Thriving organizations have magnetism," he says.) Are we attracting nice, conscientious people to be students here?
- Do students feel more fully alive as a result of being at the school? Do they feel belonging? Do they come early? Do they stay late? Do they come to the optional events? Do they feel that they're contributing to the community?
- Is it absolutely evident that we value the team? Do staff members feel listened to? Are they autonomous? Do teachers laugh together? Do they talk socially? ("If the staff members are thriving, the students feel that.")

These are the indicators that let AJ know the conditions are in place for life to thrive at every level – for students, for staff, for the school itself, for the community. Not coincidentally, he senses a strong connection between this set of indicators and the school's profitability – a tangible, quantifiable measure of its health.

And here's where a note of caution is needed. What would be the effect if AJ introduced personality tests as part of the application process, in an effort to measure how "nice and conscientious" new students are? Imagine if he set targets for how often students arrive early for class, giving teachers bonuses for surpassing those objectives. What if he closely monitored the number of times teachers laugh together, charting and posting the results each week? Here's where we have to ask: What would be altered or diminished through measurement?

Importantly, the greatest value is often not in the measures themselves but in engaging people in identifying those indicators, building awareness, connection, discovery and commitment in the process. This is why several of the stories throughout this section feature a broadly participatory process to craft a manifesto – the story of who they are together, what they want, and what has to be true if they are to get what they want. Such an exercise helps people identify the necessary fertile conditions and indicators that will let them know they're evolving in ways they want to.

In personal correspondence, Gil Friend, Chief Sustainability Officer for the City of Palo Alto, suggested that what is needed is to "make a business transparent to all its participants. With 'open book management' (and OMG perhaps even broad ownership) the participants will decide and learn and decide again where their attention and interventions can be most usefully placed."

In the same correspondence, organizational consultant and fellow living systems pioneer Max Skhud added to this, proposing a shift from asking "How do we introduce effective metrics?" to "How do we design highly generative feedback loops throughout the system, embedded in the fabric of our everyday operations, that would support us in evolving toward more thriving/aliveness at every level of [the] system?"

The Community Mastery Board

In one small example of such an embedded feedback loop, multi-talented entrepreneur Arthur Brock introduced what he calls "Community Mastery Boards" at the Agile Learning Center schools he and others have pioneered in several locations. Taking inspiration from Agile software development practices like Kanban and Scrum, the practice involves a weekly brief meeting involving students, teachers and staff. At the heart of the meeting is a white board with four columns drawn on it: Noticing, Implementing, Practicing, and Mastery. If someone notices something they would like to bring to the attention of the community, they create a sticky note about it and place it in the

Noticing column. The group discusses the issue, quickly brainstorms possible solutions and chooses one solution to implement on a test basis for the next week. The original sticky note plus another with the proposed solution are placed in the Implementing column. If at the next meeting the prototyped solution seems to be effective, the two sticky notes are advanced to the Practicing column and the community moves into practicing this new behavior on its way to adopting it as an ongoing practice. Eventually, the issue and solution are moved into the Mastery column as it is integrated as a cultural norm.

Nancy Tilton, founder of the Agile Learning Center in Charlotte, North Carolina, recounted the process in action:

> At the beginning of the year, slamming doors was a big problem. Our doors are big and heavy and the hinges slam them shut. Without intending to, it is really easy to create a very loud slam with very little force. This is not pleasant to hear all day! We added this to our [Noticing] column: "Slamming Doors." Then each week, we check in, "Have you guys been hearing the doors slam a lot or is this getting better?" The act of just asking and then celebrating with the students each week on this has made this occurrence happen less and less. What I am celebrating currently is that every time the door does get accidentally slammed now, the person who did it almost ALWAYS pops their head back in the room with a meek, "I'm sorry." That means a lot as a community – we will all slip-up, but acknowledging that our intent was not to disrupt others and apologizing goes a long way.[108]

This is a simple example of designing for ongoing feedback and response. It supports that community in growing into thrivability in large and small ways. (Visit www.agilelearningcenters.org for more resources and design examples.)

In all, as we consider the question of measuring thrivability, the goal is not to be able to declare that "Our organization is 73% thrivable," or "Our thrivability is up 17% over last quarter." Nor will it ever be possible to pronounce that "The organization is now thrivable," as if it is a *fait accompli*. Instead, the goal is to explore how we can develop widely distributed sensitivity and responsiveness to both tangible and intangible aspects of the system so the story can move ever forward in the direction of more thriving – more expressiveness, connectedness, generativity and healing - for more of the organizational ecosystem.

In other words, the ultimate objective of measurement and sensing is to make the flow of life discernible so we can respond to that information with effective stewardship.

3.11

STORY #5: CRUDESSENCE

[Written by Julian Giacomelli, CEO of Crudessence at the time of writing in December 2012. The company is a successful Montreal-based food services company with multiple restaurants, a catering business, an academy, and in-store and online sales of prepared foods and related products.]

A T CRUDESSENCE, WE feel very strongly about sustainability and strive to go even beyond to transcend the commonly held vision of sustainability. Coming from deep in our collective values is the belief that there is a new way to be in business, in community and in life. And we are out to live that vision.

The company has grown significantly in many ways over the past five years, and in good part due to our expanding diversity. Diversity in the customer base, the employee pool and even in our offering. We have grown over ten times in that period. As the reach and size of our ecosystem has grown, what was once a clear vision among a handful of employees started to become less so. We started hearing disagreements among staff and confusion from our customers as to what Crudessence was all about. There was a growing and apparent need to clarify and perhaps expand on the original vision of the founders, who had strong intentions, but had not imagined the size of this endeavour. So we decided to undertake a vision quest for Crudessence, and set out to create a manifesto.

In expressing a manifesto, we hoped there would be numerous rich benefits along the way and that a manifesto would surely contribute in ways we did not know and could not name. We realized that an organism cannot mature into vibrant health if it does not fully know who or what it is. The calling for a collaborative self-expression of Crudessence was clear. So the journey began, with a firm belief that this endeavour would kick-start a new phase in our development.

With the guidance and leadership of visionary Michelle Holliday (Thrivability Montreal and Cambium) and über-consultant/coach Jean-Philippe Bouchard (Spiralis), we embarked on what would turn out to be a nearly one-year manifesto-crafting journey. Through dialogue with multiple stakeholders, we tackled topics found in a typical visioning or mission-definition exercise, and we also touched on more subtle layers, calling for an inner organizational voice to emerge. We wanted to touch basic existential questions like who we are and what we want to be, and to listen for what else seemed alive in us.

In the process design, we simultaneously founded the Crudessence Community of Stewards (CoS), a leadership group comprised of the founders, managers, connectors and coordinators. The intention behind the CoS was to create a community of learning and sharing among the leaders, or "stewards," of Crudessence. We have met roughly every three to four months since December 2011.

At the initial offsite meeting, we prepared "data" for the stewards to look at, asking Crudessence to express itself through the various lenses of the clients, the organization, the money, the staff and the community. We spent 36 hours ruminating on what we were grateful for, what brought us together, what held us back, and we all shared much more. From this meeting, the seeds for the manifesto were sown.

Following this, we invited all our staff to a series of half-day meetings, at which we shared stories, played games and expressed what we loved and liked less about Crudessence. We talked about what we aspired to be and what we wanted to avoid. We shared food and laughed, inviting other stakeholders to the meetings, including key suppliers and trusted customers. The harvest was sifted through, combined with information from the past, and a small group started writing. Through a number of iterations of feedback from the founders, CoS, and staff at large, the manifesto slowly emerged, at a natural pace. The final draft was agreed upon in September.

The manifesto now graces the walls of our Academy, the Crudessence website and our restaurant menus, and it has been shared through social media into our ecosystem. Over the next few months, we will post it in all the physical Crudessence spaces and continue to improve it. It serves as a rallying point, as marching orders, a flag to carry, and a clear expression of what we aim to do - and how we strive to be. It can help us recruit staff and partners better, and speak to our customers in precise language.

When something comes from deep within you, it is as if it was always there. I already cannot remember what Crudessence was like before the manifesto.

3.12

THE VITAL ROLE OF DEATH

I T SEEMS APPROPRIATE to close our exploration of thrivability with a chapter about the role of death.

The common misconception is that thrivability is all about peak experience – vibrant health and joy, all the time. Rainbows and unicorns all the way.

For some, this can be very appealing. In all of today's stress and distress, many are drawn to the idea of feeling constantly happy and connected within their organization, of non-stop smooth collaboration, of feeling clarity and progress without end. They are then disappointed and disillusioned the first moment they realize this is not a reality that can be supported for long.

For others, the misconception can have the opposite effect, turning them away at the very outset with the assumption that such Pollyanna promises can't possibly be true. And, of course, they are right, in part.

Full, vibrant health and joy clearly can't be our sustained state for all time. We know that life also includes death. And conflict. It includes confusion, challenges and difficult emotions. In nature, there are seasons. There are ebbs and flows. There is day and also night. These are not unwanted, yet unavoidable aspects of life; they are necessary and useful. Within the practice of thrivability, they offer particularly fertile grounds. And they must be embraced as a vital part of stewarding any system's thrivability.

To illustrate this, I'll share a simple – if slightly embarrassing – story of how I learned this lesson in my recent adventures as an amateur gardener.

It all started with one innocent-looking packet of basil seeds, an investment of under $3. For the first time, I had decided to try my hand at growing something from seeds. The experiment took place on the sunny little second-story balcony outside my home office. As I scattered the impossibly tiny black dots into several seedling trays in late spring, I noticed that it seemed like a lot of seeds. But I didn't give it much further thought; I was focused instead on imagining the taste of fresh pesto.

Two weeks later, each of the nine little pods in about as many seedling trays was suddenly crammed with tiny light green leaves. Clearly, they already needed more space. So whenever I could steal away from work and family, I would transfer one pod's worth – 8 or 10 delicate little sprouts – into separate small pots, giving each tiny plant its own space. But there were so many of them! And I only had so many pots and so much soil, and it was a time-consuming process. So I went out and bought more pots and more soil. And evening after evening, I would leave my children to fend for themselves temporarily as I squatted on the dirt-covered floor of the balcony, transferring tiny sprouts into their own little pots. Within days, I noticed that the transferred sprouts had quickly grown too big for their new pots! It turns out that they grew in proportion to the space available (as life seems to do). And so again, I had to go buy more, larger pots and more soil.

In what I knew was a ridiculous situation, by mid-July, my little balcony was close to overflowing with over 100 pots of varying sizes, each with its own still-diminutive sprout or seedling. This was *far* more than I had bargained for. And I couldn't imagine how *any* of them would ever grow to the size of the big bushy plants at the grocery store. Jealously, I tried to console myself – those plants cost $3 <u>each</u>, and I had over

100 plants for that price! But I knew I was fooling myself. What was worse, I still had an overwhelming number of trays of crowded tiny sprouts I hadn't yet gotten to – and that hadn't grown any bigger in all these weeks. My kids were starting to complain that I loved the basil more than I loved them. And truly, I *do* love pesto. But this whole basil experiment was really not working.

For help and advice, I turned to my landscape architect friend, Adam. Gently, he told me it was better not to transplant all the seedlings from each pod – only the tallest and strongest one. That I had to make *choices*. That none of them would thrive if I didn't. It's a question of resources, he said. Of creating "space for life." I shared with Adam that this was difficult emotionally – those little plants looked so eager and full of potential. "I appreciate your empathy," he wrote, "but nature is really quite explicit about this sort of thing."

For some things to thrive, some others may have to die. For the system overall to thrive, there may have to be multiple experiments, from which only some are chosen. And there may be things that have come to their natural end and must be turned back to compost, in turn nourishing the rest of the system.

In each of those circumstances, **death is a generative act**. Paradoxically, it is a vital part of thrivability.

My friend and Non-Violent Communication trainer, Valérie Lanctôt-Bédard, talks about giving birth to some things and also "giving death" to others, in a generous spirit. The Berkana Institute's Deborah Frieze has pioneered a "two-loop model" that recognizes the need at once to hospice the old and to give birth to the new.[109] Another friend, Vanessa Reid, writes eloquently about hospicing the magazine she edited, engaging in a collective practice of "conscious closure" after ten years of publication:

> This experience taught us how important it is to make conscious the need
> to foresee and steward endings in organizations. Endings are the compost for

new beginnings, new visions and paradigms – and certainly the compost for new life. We cannot pour more water in an already full cup, so clearing the space to bring in the new is essential.

We learned the importance of, and created **a personal and an organizational practice** around, cultivating the patience and ability to hold the paradoxes of celebration and grieving, of doing good work together and doing our final work together. We were simultaneously letting something go AND in the creative process of producing a **legacy** (in the form of the 10th Anniversary issue of ascent magazine). Holding these paradoxes and these seemingly divergent emotions was a core capacity we cultivated – and if our organizations are truly "organismes" [the French word for organization], then we need to FEEL them, rather than simply strategize around them.[110]

We see this spirit of embracing the role of death in the rising popularity of "rapid prototyping" and in calls to "fail fast." There is even a growing trend to issue annual Failure Reports, pioneered by Engineers Without Borders in 2009. The Stanford Social Innovation Review even wrote an article about it called "Thriving on Failure." In an organizational world that until recently viewed endings and death as cause for deep shame, these practices signal important progress.

Such forays into "stewarding death" open the door for a compelling question from Vanessa: *What skills and structures are needed to hold the space for creative destruction and renewal?*

Another friend, author Will Walker, cautions on "the subtlety of what we load [thrivability] with."

[We] all have preferences of what we perceive could be "thriving" or not. Some of us are very comfortable in the alive movements of life and less comfortable in the dying away of life. Some less comfortable in the movement and more comfortable in the surrendering. Both are important.

Tolu Ilesanmi, CEO of Zenith Cleaning, has shared with me how this is a challenge for his staff. There have been times when they want to move forward and do innovative things, whereas he feels the organization needs to come back to the company's ground of practice: embodying cleaning. To lose this ground would be to lose the depth of the message. Stewardship, in that case, means letting those new initiatives die – or pruning them back – to leave space for the more foundational work of cleaning as practice.

What seems to be needed most at these times is recognition that "giving death" is a vital part of stewarding an organization's ongoing evolution. What is needed is the care and courage to make a compassion-filled space for that process. Not only will this create a more human organization, it stands to enable renewal and innovation, to enhance learning, and to deepen relationships and relational capacity – positive outcomes by any standard. The ultimate benefit, however, is that **every organization may become a practice ground for grace**.

At the time of writing (late July), I'm down to 30 or so basil plants. They're getting nice and big, thanks to the soil and space freed up by the seedlings and sprouts I didn't carry forward (and whose tiny leaves seasoned several meals).

The experience gave me an easy, tangible lesson about the practice of stewardship and the vital role of death.

And happily, fresh pesto is now clearly in my future.

SECTION 4

MOVING INTO THE AGE OF THRIVABILITY

4.1

THE NEED FOR PRACTICE GROUNDS

H OW DO WE actively embrace our organizations and communities as living systems and work to cultivate thriving within them? How do we move forward into the Age of Thrivability that the living systems patterns suggest is just within reach?

Part of the answer is: follow the signs. A path forward is becoming clear, as pioneers lead the way. In cities around the world, there is a positive frenzy of activity around "social innovation" – new, systemic approaches to problems that plague society at large. Participatory organizational models and life-affirming investment methods are sprouting up *and* flourishing. Communities are being gathered and stewarded in novel ways, inviting unprecedented levels of inclusion, connection and creativity. Young people, in particular, are jumping into action to change the way things are done. Experimental spaces are being created – social labs, festivals, art hives, fab labs – in which the new story can be tested and experienced. And the language of living systems thinking is present throughout, with concepts like resilience, ecosystems, emergence and agility as the implicit mantras of the movement.

Within this flurry of new practices, there are countless examples of relatively small design changes that can have a surprisingly large impact, creating the conditions for what futurist Venessa Miemis calls "emergence by design." Short daily stand-up meetings within the Agile movement offer inspiration, for example, with everyone sharing what they've done, what they intend to do that day, and where they need help. The Community Mastery Board described in Chapter 3.10 offers a similarly simple, but powerful tweak to the way things are done. When he took over a struggling alternative school (which would later become the first Agile Learning Center), Arthur Brock made participation in governance meetings optional; this set a whole new tone, as well as clearing a path to more effective action. My colleague Kim Fuller, founder of Phil Communications, got culture change rolling within a particularly dysfunctional client organization by overseeing redecoration of the staff kitchen and meeting room, making those spaces more conducive to conversation and community. In my own experience, I've seen dramatic shifts come from changing the physical structure of a meeting from a board room table to an open circle of chairs. Likewise, the practice of checking in and checking out of meetings, so every voice is heard, can have significant effect. Small, targeted changes to the design of interactions can pave the way for greater openness, creativity and momentum.

At the same time, the more substantive challenge is that those design changes must be accompanied by changes in *thinking*, in *perspective*, in *consciousness*, or they won't stick and they won't have the full desired impact.

And so I would also say that, "The answer to *how* is *yes*," as bestselling author Peter Block advises in his marvelous book of that title. If thrivability is in some ways about following the energy of "yes" on its own terms, noticing and nourishing life as it shows up, then Block advises us that, "Transformation comes more from pursuing profound questions than seeking practical answers."[111] Rather than rushing into action (or perhaps *alongside* the action), there is value in reflection, in talking with others and checking in with your own understanding, intentions and assumptions, in plumbing the deeper implications of this new story of organization. "For the human species to evolve," Margaret Mead observed, "the conversation must deepen."

Because every living system is unique, there will likely be relatively little that can be prescribed and limited value in prescription. The much more significant benefit – whether in an organization or a community – comes in the awareness, connection, discovery and commitment that result from time spent reflecting together on what is needed most. An invitation-based, broadly participatory process of discerning and developing opportunities is as important as the opportunities themselves, enriching the community through learning and relationship. A strategic plan *will* take shape. A path to positive change *will* become clear. But it will be richer, wiser and more comprehensive than you could have imagined, rooted as it will be in a compelling story, in people's passions and in place. Even more importantly, an engaged, activated and thriving community will emerge along the way.

Julie Bourbonnais describes such an approach at Space for Life, the complex of four Montreal-based nature museums that were merged administratively by the city:

> We actually listened to what was in the center – to what the organization wanted to tell us, what does it want to become.... What we heard was that there's something really important to be done.... It was to become not only individual spaces for life. Each individual institution is a space for life. In all its beauty, it's how do we create awe and invite care so that we all together are one huge space for life. It was to invite people to love and protect and create spaces for life in their own environment, home, garden or school. It became something so much bigger than just who we were. That vision sustained the passion and the innovation, and it's still going on today. Are things perfect? No. But that heroic cause keeps people mobilized even when they get discouraged.[112]

As we consider the question of "how," what is called for, then, is not an all-purpose checklist or a set of best practices (though these may come in handy). Instead, what is most called for is an **action-learning orientation**, enabling people to listen and respond to the unfolding story of the organization as it happens. What is needed is an ongoing and active practice of stewardship.

At the heart of this practice is the cultivation of courage. Courage to try new things, certainly. To experiment, learn and sometimes fail. But there is something more. Perhaps even more than "life after death," it seems to take courage to believe in "life *before* death." To believe you may be part of an epic narrative of vibrant aliveness. That you may have a special role to play. That life might be truly beautiful. It takes courage to open your heart to those possibilities, knowing your heart may be broken along the way. It's so much easier to deny the imagination, to remain cynical and closed, to settle for the familiar outlines of the incremental and transactional. But as Anaïs Nin shared of her own experience: "The day came when the risk to remain tight in a bud was more painful than the risk it took to blossom." For many, that day has come. The pain is in us and in the world. And we need each other if we are to find the courage to blossom.

If we are to cultivate this type of practice, then we have to create time and space for it, both individually and collectively. We need to create our own "spaces for life" – practice fields where we can reflect and renew, like plants taken in to a nourishing greenhouse for a time. As Vanessa Reid recounts:

I've been in many conversations with people in Canada and in my international network about the kinds of learning spaces that are needed now, ones that are integrated into an enlarged life, as the poet John O'Donohue writes, and where place and its stories have a place at the table, so to speak, as a teacher, not a consumable item.

There is a deep need for reflective space when there is such acceleration, complexity, urgency. The quality of our presence to ourselves, each other, to life, IS the work. This is the container for sustaining social innovation. These are the spaces, in other words, that simply sustain us on the big ride with life as it shows up.

Innovation, for me, is a life practice. It starts with how we connect to the "kefi" as they say in Greek, the life force. And once in tune with that, there is life that comes through us that allows the new to be seen. And sometimes, by a trick of the light, and as I wrote in my little poem, "there are very old things in the birthing of the new" so the newest shiny things are actually the essential gems that last and get re-discovered all over again.[113]

As you dedicate such time and space to the practice of stewardship and the ongoing cultivation of thrivability – either in your organization or community – certain conditions will be most fertile:

- A field of action (something to steward, a practice ground, for example, a community project or your organization) – something bounded and purposeful and larger than yourself.

- Rootedness in the mythic story and geography of place – like plants, we and our projects require the soil of a particular place.

- A community of fellow action-learners:

  - Each of whom has a commitment to developing their own capacity to steward life, to listen for what is needed and to be of service.

  - With a shared commitment to being in healthy, open relationship and communication.

  - Ideally, united by love of a place and its community, which opens the door to the creation of shared fields of action.

- A regular, repeated rhythm of ample blocks of time for reflection and renewal. We need not to accelerate but to expand our experience of time, so within it we can develop our ability to sense what is needed and to feel our own aliveness.

- Practices for hosting participatory, generative conversations, both within the action and within separate times of reflection and renewal. (Search online for the Art of Hosting, the Applied Improv Network and Liberating Structures for information about a wide range of such practices.)

- The necessary nourishment of nature, physical movement, creativity, the arts, beauty and music.

These are the ingredients of regular gatherings for the Community of Stewards within Crudessence, for all members of the Enspiral network and for the Agile Learning Centers. Many of these are present in regular, extended staff meetings at Zenith Cleaners and CLC. And they are the core characteristics of Solarium practice groups that my colleague Michael Jones and I host.

Within these fertile conditions, you will be well supported as you respond to stewardship's "four callings," engaging in any or all of these generative conversations, or variations of them that seem relevant and timely to you:

- What more could it mean at this moment in time for each of us, individually, to be able to bring the best of ourselves? To feel deeply at home in this place, in this work and in our own bodies? And what could support that?
- What more could it mean at this moment in time for our infrastructure and interactions to support not only information sharing, decision-making, effective action and trust but playfulness, learning and joy? For our patterns of belonging with colleagues, customers and community to be infused with a sense of dedication, earnestness, perhaps even sacredness? And what could support that?
- What more do we understand at this moment in time about the calling or purpose – the emergent, unifying story – that propels us into transformative action together, as citizens, employees, customers, community members? What new possibilities are now apparent for how we will craft and live into that story of wholeness and wonder?
- How else can we integrate the first three conditions, ensuring coherence across all of them? And in all of them, how can we be inspired, nourished and renewed by nature, beauty, art, music, movement and celebration? How

can we allow life to flow through us, so the new may be seen, or the essential gems rediscovered? How can we truly savor this experience of being alive?

Even without a group to gather with and regular, ample blocks of time and space – without a dedicated Solarium of your own – there is value and insight available simply in journaling about these questions, reflecting on them during a morning walk, or engaging someone else in thoughtful conversation about them.

Our greatest challenge is not lack of answers to these questions. The world has exploded with new, life-aligned strategies and tactics, and even more discovery awaits us in our conversations and imaginings. Instead, the real challenge is to find the collective will and courage to ask the questions, to embark on these new paths, to create space and time to learn from the journey, and to focus not only on changing our systems, but on changing ourselves along the way. In a world that tells us that busyness and productivity are their own reward and that thriving is not a reasonable goal, the core challenge is to believe in our own worthiness and ability to thrive.

4.2

WHAT BECOMES POSSIBLE

BEYOND THE DETAILS of patterns, models, archetypes and designs, this book has most of all charted the emergence of a new guiding story, one in which we can more clearly see and cultivate the qualities of aliveness in our organizations, in our communities, and in ourselves.

Indeed, fundamentally reconceiving the organization and our role within it is the most powerful "social innovation" possible. This is systems scientist Donella Meadows' premise that the highest leverage point within a system is changing the guiding paradigm.[114]

To move into an Age of Thrivability, we need to look up to see the landscape stretching out ahead of us, the horizon beckoning from the distance. We need to see ourselves more fully as active stewards of life's unfolding process and as part of a larger living world.

With this broader view, we can see that our organizations have the potential to be places where we are nourished by our relationships and by the opportunity to contribute and develop our gifts. Where we can be held appreciatively by people and place. Where we can experience beauty, wholeness and healing within our communities and our workplaces. Where we can grow into wisdom alongside each other, with trust that this is the most direct path to effective action. And where these are the express purposes of coming together.

Indeed, **the organization is poised to be transformed from the too-often toxic workplace to the sacred temple of our times.**

To imagine this, of course, we have to expand what we think of as a temple – from a rare, secluded place with special architecture and prescribed rituals and rules, to any space made sacred by those who engage within it in the spirit of stewarding life.

We can be helped in this expansion of thought by an inspiring short documentary about the Guardians of the Temple of Transition, a structure that is built and set ablaze each year at the Burning Man festival in the Black Rock Desert of Nevada. In this case, the word "guardian" mirrors "steward" quite closely. "The Guardian is a role," film-maker Ian MacKenzie explains. "Living cultures throughout the world have known the importance of Guardians – those that hold the space for ritual and rites of passage, for death and the welcoming of new life." Within the film, one of the Temple Guardians explains: "It's only when people start filling it with their grief and their love that then it becomes a temple."[115]

This is the larger vision of stewardship, and the larger potential of our organizations and communities – that they will offer fertile containers to hold both our grief and our love and to welcome new patterns of life. That they will guide us into an Age of Thrivability.

Importantly, all of this is not a call to communism or capitalism, to individualism or collectivism, to indigenous Earth-based spirituality or the technological drive toward progress, to valuing love or money, to action or reflection. Instead, it is a call to a transcendent "third way" that encompasses each of these dualities. It is a move into an era of integration, leading to new ways of seeing and being. This is a path to much richer meaning and connection. To the compassion and collaboration we'll need to solve humanity's most persistent and threatening problems. To bridging fragmented approaches. To moving beyond compromises that stop short of what's really needed.

As Julie Bourbonnais, former Assistant Director of Space for Life, notes:

Thrivability is foremost ... wanting things to be better, to endure with time, joyfully, meaningfully. It's about knowing that what you're doing is meaningful and will contribute to life, to something being alive. It's not easy. It's not paradise. It brings up hard questions and hard work. It calls for a new way of thinking. But it's the only reasonable way, if we're really honest with ourselves.[116]

This book has sought to offer an abundance of reason – probably far more than is needed. I hope it has also inspired even a small amount of reverence as the most potent pathway into a thoughtful and genuine practice of stewardship. It is our reverence, more than our reason, that will allow us to love and believe in ourselves enough to do what's really needed... that will guide us in cherishing the Earth as our larger self... that will help us nurture each other ... and that will enable us to honor and trust life enough to settle into grace.

In these ways, thrivability represents even more than new perspectives and practices. Thrivability is a quest. A hero's journey. A choose-your-own-adventure story. The challenges we face in our organizations and in the world call for nothing less. And our own hearts crave nothing more.

There is much more to write and more to explore. May this book serve as one of many useful guides as we move into an Age of Thrivability.

Resources

INVITE YOU TO visit *www.ageofthrivability.com*, a site where you can:

- Discover articles, slideshows, videos, practices and stories;
- Talk about the concepts in this book, connect with others, deepen your understanding, contribute your stories, make connections with other models, tools and perspectives, explore, experiment and play with the concepts.
- Find out about upcoming events.

Also, the following communities may be useful in your practice of stewardship (they have been for me):

- There is a global community of practice called the Art of Hosting and Harvesting Conversations that Matter, teaching a range of participatory meeting techniques to catalyze the purpose and passion – the life – that brings people together.
- OpenSpace Agility is a straightforward methodology for effectively introducing culture change through engagement, game mechanics, leadership storytelling and more.
- The Applied Improvisation Network uses playful methods to help people achieve shared intentions and to unleash creativity and life along the way.
- Non-Violent Communication is a widespread practice that enables people to express their individual needs within healthy relationship.
- The Social Lab process brings together the full social ecosystem affected by a shared challenge, in shared experimentation and learning.

What underlies each of these approaches is implicit recognition of the life in our communities and our organizations – and of the aliveness of the world around us. All of them are being used to resolve conflicts and heal situations of violence, to open up new possibilities, and to invite people into new chapters in the human story. And there are many more such approaches. There is no shortage of ways to create the conditions for life to thrive wherever humans gather.

Acknowledgements

A FTER WORKING ON this book for more than a decade, I can't possibly name all the people who have influenced and inspired it and who have supported me along the way. Here is a small sampling of those to whom I feel deep gratitude:

To the original paradigm pioneers who have inspired me for decades: Margaret Wheatley, Elisabet Sahtouris, Peter Senge, Peter Block, Fritjof Capra, Arie de Geus and others.

To Michael Jones, whose foreword described the book I hadn't yet realized I wanted to write, inspiring me to adapt and expand my original manuscript, and for being such an enchanting collaborator and friend.

To the amazing Montreal gang of thrivability pioneers and dear friends: Julie Bourbonnais, Tolu Ilesanmi, Sophie Derevianko, Julian Giacomelli, AJ Javier, Sonia Di Maulo, William Walker, Seb Paquet, Samantha Slade (and the whole Percolab gang), Jean-Philippe Bouchard, Valerie Lanctôt-Bédard, Kim Fuller and many more, for love, encouragement and shared learning, and for your beautiful spirits. You've made Montreal my home.

To the global Art of Hosting community for so much generosity and shared learning about creating space for life.

To Belina Raffy, for teaching me so much about practical play, fantastic facilitation and bacon-fueled friendship, for adding tremendously to the thrivability framework, and for leading the Thrivable World Quest so saucily.

To Anne Paré, for generously crafting the original cover design, and for the compassion and beauty you radiate.

To Tara-Lee Duffy and Vanessa Reid, for being magical sprites of boldness and delight who, to me, embody the practice of thrivability.

To Daniel Mezick, for reading and commenting on this book's manuscript in great (and enthusiastic) detail, for developing and generously sharing OpenSpace Agility and teaching me about the role of authority, and for being such fun to learn and teach with.

To Bill Veltrop and Ben Roberts, for being constant cheerleaders and connectors, both for me personally and for a more life-centered worldview.

To Peter Pula, Ben Wolfe and the Axiom team, for friendship and faith in me – and in what the charming little village of Peterborough, Ontario, has to show the world.

To Adam Clack, for carefully reading the manuscript – more than once – and offering invaluable feedback and encouragement, and for generously giving us a living practice ground.

To Marina Nacheva and John Riley, for your love, support and long years of friendship.

To Jean Russell, for leading the thrivability charge so wisely and generously all these years.

To George (and Mary!) Foster, for bringing your immense cover design talents to my beloved book. Pure magic.

To Willy Mathes, for masterful editorial work and thoughtful, wise coaching. What could have been a painful process was instead a delight. You are truly a gem.

To my mother, Susan Holliday, for being the original and constant visionary, and for always being available to listen and encourage, even in your darkest hours. *Who's had my back for 45 years?*

To my husband, Alan Clack, for more than a decade of selfless support and sacrifice, all because you wanted me to be happy. I am. Thank you.

To my children, Sunny and Dylan, for snuggles, laughter and love and for being almost as proud of me as I am of you. This is for you.

ABOUT THE AUTHOR

For nearly two decades, visionary thought leader Michelle Holliday has written and presented on the future of society. As a facilitator and consultant, her work centers around "thrivability" – a set of perspectives, intentions, and practices based on a view of organizations and communities as dynamic living systems.

She spent the first part of her career in brand strategy, working internationally for Coca-Cola and H.J. Heinz. The second part of her career focused on employee engagement, consulting for a variety of organizations in Washington, DC. Now, she combines both disciplines as founder of Montreal-based Cambium Consulting, working with a range of pioneering clients.

Michelle has a master's degree with a concentration in international marketing and a bachelor's degree in Russian studies. She has lived in nineteen cities around the world, including Moscow, London, Paris, and a small town in Scotland. She now lives in Montreal with her husband and two children.

ENDNOTES

1   Michelle Holliday, "The Practice of Thrivability" Posted February 11, 2011 http://solarium.cambiumconsulting.com/content/what-thrivability

2   Joanna Macy, general welcome message on website. Accessed August 18, 2011 http://www.joannamacy.net/

3   Michael Lissak and Johan Roos. *The Next Common Sense: The e-Manager's Guide to Mastering Complexity* (London: Nicholas Brealey Publishing, 1999) p. 1.

4   Todd Sattersten, "More Space: Nine Antidotes to Complacency in Business" Astronaut Projects, 2005.

5   Thomas Petzinger, Jr. *The New Pioneers: The Men and Women Who are Transforming the Workplace and Marketplace* (New York: Simon & Schuster, 1999) p. 23.

6   Howard Bloom, *The Lucifer Principle: An Expedition into the Forces of History* (Grove/Atlantic, 1995) p. 58.

7   David Loye, "Telling the New Story" July 8, 2004. Accessed September 8, 2010 http://www.thedarwinproject.com/adventure/newstory/newstory.pdf p.6.

8   Donald Ingber, "The Architecture of Life" *Scientific American*, January 1998, p.48.

9   Michael Colebrook, "Emergence" Posted January 30, 2013. Accessed September 8, 2014 http://greenspirit.org.uk/resourcepack/?p=1029

10 W. Edwards Deming, *The New Economics*, Second edition: Chapter 4. Accessed February 26, 2008 http://deming.org/index.cfm?content=66

11 Peter Senge, *The Fifth Discipline: The Art and Practice of the Learning Organization* (Currency DoubleDay, 2006) p. 7.

12   Ibid, p. 397.

13   Alan B. Scrivener, "A Curriculum for Cybernetics and Systems Theory" March 4, 2012. Accessed September 12, 2014 http://www.well.com/user/abs/curriculum.html#Defined

14   Eric D. Beinhocker, *The Origin of Wealth: Evolution, Complexity, and the Radical Remaking of Economics* (Cambridge: Harvard Business Press, 2006).

15   Humberto Maturana and Francisco Varela, *Autopoiesis and Cognition: The Realization of the Living* (D. Reidel Publishing, 1980), p. 76.

16   Bruce Millett, "Understanding Organisations: The Dominance of Systems Theory" *International Journal of Organisational Behaviour*, 1(1), 1-12. Accessed October 14, 2009 http://www.usq.edu.au/extrafiles/business/journals/hrmjournal/internationalarticles/domofsystemstheorymillett.pdf

17   Steve Jong, "Musing on Metrics: Why Measure Usability?" Reprinted from *Usability Interface*, Vol. 7, No. 2, October 2000. Accessed September 8, 2014 http://www.stcsig.org/usability/newsletter/0010-metrics.html

18   Tibor Ganti, *The Principles of Life* (Oxford: Oxford University Press, 2003) p. 2. Accessed January 31, 2016 https://books.google.ca/books?id=pdVU8mpWNWYC&pg=PA3&lpg=PA3&dq=Living+systems+are+chemical+automata&source=bl&ots=mLLCub_J6p&sig=z8lqIj89ZFtV5eF2weFXMF6jZGQ&hl=en&sa=X&ved=0ahUKEwjqpLCb0tTKAhXRsh4KHdYdDEIQ6AEIHDAA#v=onepage&q=Living%20systems%20are%20chemical%20automata&f=false

19   N.A.R. Gow, G.D. Robson and G.M. Gadd (editors), *The Fungal Colony* (Cambridge University Press, 1999). Specific citation: Chapter 1: "Self-integration – an emerging concept from the fungal mycelium" by A.D.M. Rayner, Z.R. Watkins and J.R. Beeching.

20 Jack McClintock, "This is Your Ancestor" *Discover Magazine*, November 2004. Accessed September 13, 2011 http://discovermagazine.com/2004/nov/this-is-your-ancestor

21 Chris Lucas, "Autopoiesis and Coevolution." Accessed April 14, 2016 http://www.neuroredes.com.br/site/artigos/autopoiesis_and_coevolution.htm

22 Per Bak, *How Nature Works: The Science of Self-Organised Criticality* (New York: Copernicus Press, 1996).

23 David Pratt, "Theosophy and the Systems View of Life" Accessed September 8, 2014 http://www.theosophy-nw.org/theosnw/science/prat-sys.htm

24 Fritjof Capra, *The Turning Point* (Berkeley, California: Shambala, 2000) p. 288.

25 Lyall Watson, *Supernature II* (Sceptre, 1987) p. 24.

26 Cited by M. Allen Cooperstein in "The Conjoint Evolution of Creativity and Consciousness: A Developmental Perspective" Accessed September 8, 2014 http://www.wynja.com/personality/candc.html

27 Stuart Kauffman, *At Home in the Universe: The Search for the Laws of Self-Organization* (Oxford University Press: 1995) p. vii.

28 David Pratt. "Theosophy and the Systems View of Life." Accessed September 8, 2014 http://www.theosophy-nw.org/theosnw/science/prat-sys.htm

29 Janis Birkeland (editor), *Design for Sustainability: A Sourcebook of Integrated Eco-Logical Solutions* (London, England: Earthscan Publications, 2002) Chapter written by Kath Wellman, p. 75.

30 Vaclav Havel, "The Need for Transcendence in the PostModern World" Speech given at Independence Hall, July 4, 1994. Accessed September 12, 2014 http://www.worldtrans.org/whole/havelspeech.html

31   Karen Schomer, Letter to the editor, *Business Week*. November 22, 1999.

32   Bruce G. Charlton, "What is the Meaning of Life? Animism, Generalised Anthropomorphism and Social Intelligence" 2002. Accessed September 8, 2014. http://www.hedweb.com/bgcharlton/meaning-of-life.html

33   Christopher McDougall, *Born to Run: A Hidden Tribe, Superathletes, and the Greatest Race the World Has Never Seen* (Knopf, 2009).

34   The Paranormal Investigation and Research Group. Accessed September 9, 2014 https://sites.google.com/site/paranormalirgsite/home/paranormal-dictionary/-a-page-2

35   Gayle Highpine, "Need good definition for shamanism/shamanic practice" *Tribe*, January 28, 2008. Accessed November 4, 2014 http://shamanism.tribe.net/thread/ad93ee11-42c5-4ad6-919a-5ac3b9799646

36   Bruce G. Charlton, M.D., "What is the Meaning of Life? Animism, Generalised Anthropomorphism and Social Intelligence" 2002. Accessed November 4, 2014 http://www.hedweb.com/bgcharlton/meaning-of-life.html

37   Michael Winkelman, "Shamanism and Cognitive Evolution" *Cambridge Archeological Journal*, Vol 12:1, p. 72.

38   Joseph Chilton Pearce, *Magical Child: Rediscovering Nature's Plan for our Children* (Toronto: Bantam, 1980) p. 145.

39   Orlando Patterson, *Freedom in the Making of Western Culture* (New York: Basic Books, 1991) p. 17.

40   Patterson, p. 23.

41   Bruce Charlton, M.D., "What is the Meaning of Life? Animism, Generalised Anthropomorphism and Social Intelligence" Accessed February 2, 2016   http://www.hedweb.com/bgcharlton/meaning-of-life.html

42   L.L. Whyte, *The Unconscious Before Freud* (New York: Basic Books, 1960) p. 196-197.

43   Patterson, p. 47.

44   Patterson, p. xvi.

45   Stephen D. Cox, "The Individualist Code" July 3, 2006. Accessed September 12, 2014 http://mises.org/daily/2232/

46   J.A. Ryan, "Individualism" *The Catholic Encyclopedia* (New York: Robert Appleton Company, 1910). Accessed April 14, 2016 from New Advent: http://www.newadvent.org/cathen/07761a.htm

47   Roger Scruton, "Communitarian Dreams" *City Journal*, Autumn 1996. Accessed February 7, 2012 http://www.city-journal.org/html/6_4_communitarian.html

48   James Farrell, H-Net Book Review, October 1997. Accessed April 14, 2016 http://lists.village.virginia.edu/lists_archive/sixties-l/0226.html

49   Geoff Mulgan, *Connexity: How to Live in a Connected World* (Harvard Business Review Press, 1997) p. 5.

50   Robert Putnam, *Bowling Alone: The Collapse and Revival of American Community* (New York: Simon & Schuster, 2000) p. 367.

51   Erin York Cornwell and Linda J. Waite, "Social Disconnectedness, Perceived Isolation, and Health among Older Adults" US National Library of Medicine

National Institutes of Health October 5, 2009. Accessed April 14, 2016 http://www.ncbi.nlm.nih.gov/pmc/articles/PMC2756979/

52   John Bruhn, *The Group Effect: Social Cohesion and Health Outcomes* (New York: Springer, 2009) p.13.

53   Pierre Teilhard de Chardin, *The Phenomenon of Man*, trans. Bernard Wall (New York: Harper & Row, 1965) p. 240.

54   Peter Russell, "Towards a Global Brain" July 26, 2007. Accessed April 14, 2016 http://www.peterrussell.com/GB/Chap8.php

55   Wikipedia: Gaia Hypothesis. Accessed July 23, 2014 http://en.wikipedia.org/wiki/Gaia_hypothesis

56   Paul Hawken, *Blessed Unrest: How the Largest Social Movement in History is Restoring Grace, Justice and Beauty to the World* (New York: Penguin Books, 2008). Accessed April 15, 2016 http://www.paulhawken.com/paulhawken_frameset.html

57   Peter Senge, Bryan Smith, Nina Kruschwitz, Joe Laur, Sara Schley, *The Necessary Revolution: How Individuals and Organizations are Working Together to Create a Sustainable World* (New York: Doubleday, 2008).

58   Robin Chase, "Bye-bye Capitalism. We're Entering the Age of Abundance" *Medium*, July 16, 2015. Accessed July 21, 2015 https://medium.com/backchannel/see-ya-later-capitalism-the-collaborative-economy-is-taking-over-34a5fc3a37cd

59   Paul D. MacLean, *The Triune Brain: Role in Paleocerebral Functions* (New York: Springer, 1990). Accessed October 23, 2014 http://books.google.com/books?id=4PmLFmNdHL0C&dq=Paul+D+MacLean&printsec=frontcover&source=an&hl=en&ei=SNXbS_i9JoH_8AaUqaHuBw&sa=X&oi=book_result&ct=result&resnum=10&ved=0CCcQ6AEwCQ#v=onepage&q&f=false

60   Ronald Wright, *An Illustrated Short History of Progress*. (Toronto: House of Anansi Press, 2006) p. 47.

61   Wright, p. 46.

62   Ulric Neisser, "Rising Scores on Intelligence Tests." *American Scientist*. Accessed April 26, 2012 http://www.americanscientist.org/issues/feature/rising-scores-on-intelligence-tests/9

63   Ray Kurzweil, "Where is intelligence located in the brain?" *Kurzweil: Accelerating Intelligence*. April 11, 2012. Accessed July 13, 2015 http://www.kurzweilai.net/where-is-intelligence-located-in-the-brain

64   Fred Travis, "Brain Integration Scale: Corroborating Language-based Instruments of Post-conventional Development" Abstract for the 2007 Conference of the American Psychological Association, April 24, 2007. Accessed October 23, 2014 http://www.totalbrain.ch/?page_id=42

65   Keay Davidson, "The Universe and Carl Sagan." (excerpted from *Carl Sagan: A Life*, by Keay Davidson, John Wiley & Sons, 1999) *Skeptical Inquirer*, December 1999. Accessed August 18, 2014 http://www.csicop.org/si/show/universe_and_carl_sagan/

66   Wikiquote: Buckminster Fuller. Accessed August 20, 2014 http://en.wikiquote.org/wiki/Buckminster_Fuller

67   Grant Soosalu and Marvin Oka, "Neuroscience and the Three Brains of Leadership," 2012, p. 3. Accessed July 13, 2015 http://www.leader-values.com/FCKfiles/Media/mBIT%20and%20Leadership%20article.pdf

68   Soosalu and Oka, p. 3.

69   Maria Montessori, *The Absorbent Mind* (New York: Holt, Rinehart and Winston, 1967) p. 83.

70   Deepak Chopra, from Candace Pert's *Molecules of Emotion: Why You Feel the Way You Feel* (New Caledonia: Scribner, 1997) Foreword.

71   Viktor Frankl, *Man's Search for Meaning* (Boston: Beacon Press, 1946). Accessed October 23, 2014 http://www.goodreads.com/author/quotes/2782.Viktor_E_Frankl

72   Gerry Anne Lenhart, "A Developmental Hypothesis Based on the Order of Jung's Psychological Functions: The Genesis Model" Doctoral Dissertation, submitted May 1996. Accessed October 23, 2014 http://sulcus.berkeley.edu/flm/SH/MDL/GAL/GalDisChapts/galdis.chapter1.html

73   David M Wulff, *The Psychology of Religion: Classic and Contemporary Views* (Hoboken: Wiley, 1991) p. 431.

74   "Carl Jung" NNDB. Accessed October 23, 2014 http://www.nndb.com/people/910/000031817/

75   Susanne R. Cook-Greuter, Ed.D., "Ego Development: Nine Levels of Increasing Embrace" Accessed June 19, 2009 http://www.cook-greuter.com/9%20levels%20of%20increasing%20embrace%20update%201%2007.pdf

76   Robert Jahn and Brenda Dunn, "Sensors, Filters and the Source of Reality" *Journal of Scientific Exploration*, Vol. 18, No. 4, pp 560.

77   Roger Martin, *The Opposable Mind: How Successful Leaders Win Through Integrative Thinking* (Boston, Massachusetts: Harvard Business School Press, 2007) p. 6-7.

78   Ken Wilber, *The Collected Works of Ken Wilber*, Volume 7, Introduction (Boulder, CO: Shambala Publications, 2000). Accessed October 23, 2014 http://www.fudo-mouth.net/thinktank/now_integralvision.htm

79   Buckminster Fuller, *I Seem To Be A Verb: Environment and Man's Future* (New York: Bantam Books, 1970).

80   Susanne R. Cook-Greuter, Ed.D., "Ego Development: Nine Levels of Increasing Embrace" p. 32. Accessed June 19, 2009 http://www.cook-greuter.com/9%20 levels%20of%20increasing%20embrace%20update%201%2007.pdf

81   Ibid.

82   ThinkExist: Albert Einstein Quotes. Accessed October 23, 2014 http://thinkexist. com/quotation/a_human_being_is_part_of_a_whole-called_by_us_the/10110. html

83   The Sierra Club: John Muir Misquoted. Accessed July 30, 2012 http://www.sierra-club.org/john_muir_exhibit/writings/misquotes.aspx

84   Wikiquote: Jorge Luis Borges. Accessed July 30, 2012 http://en.wikiquote.org/wiki/ Jorge_Luis_Borges

85   *Collected Works of C. G. Jung*, Vol. 9, Part 1, 2nd Ed., Princeton University Press, 1968, p. 3-41.

86   C. George Boeree. "Carl Jung" 2006. Accessed February 2, 2016 http://webspace. ship.edu/cgboer/jung.html

87   "Synchronicity" Wikipedia. Accessed February 2, 2016 https://en.wikipedia.org/ wiki/Synchronicity

88   Abraham Maslow, *Religions, Values and Peak Experiences* (Columbus: Ohio State University Press, 1976) p.33.

89   "Introduction to Transpersonal Psychology" Psychology Wiki. Accessed February 2, 2016 http://psychology.wikia.com/wiki/Introduction_to_transper-sonal_psychology

90   Tom Atlee, "Something Bigger than Life is Trying to Work Through Us" August 2009. Accessed July 30, 2012 http://co-intelligence.org/SomethingBigger.html

91   Barbara Marx Hubbard, *Emergence: The Shift From Ego to Essence* (Charlottesville, VA: Hampton Roads Publishing, 2001) p. 4.

92   Ervin Laszlo, *Chaos Point 2012 and Beyond: Appointment with Destiny* (Charlottesville, VA: Hampton Roads Publishing, 2010) pp. 39,77.

93   Jean Gebser, *The Ever-Present Origin* (Ohio University Press, 1985) p. xvii – xviii.

94   Donella H. Meadows, Dennis L. Meadows, and Jørgen Randers, "Beyond the Limits to Growth" *Context*. Accessed April 15, 2016 http://www.context.org/ICLIB/IC32/Meadows.htm

95   From a personal interview conducted in January 2015 for the Thrivable World Quest.

96   Ibid.

97   Ibid.

98   Ibid.

99   Ibid.

100 Geoff Duncan, "Why Apple stores are raking in bags full of cash, and no one can dupe the formula" *Digital Trends*, November 22, 2012. Accessed August 29, 2015   http://www.digitaltrends.com/apple/why-do-apple-stores-make-so-much-money-and-why-cant-anybody-copy-them/#ixzz3kE0cCeRa

101 From a personal interview conducted in January 2015 for the Thrivable World Quest.

102 CLC Company Website, "Who We Are." Accessed April 15, 2016 http://www.clc-montreal.com/who-we-are/

103 From a personal interview conducted in February 2015 for the Thrivable World Quest.

104 Michelle Holliday and Michael Jones. "Living Systems Theory and the Practice of Stewarding Change" *Spanda Journal*, June 2015, p. 162.

105 Robert Moore and Douglas Gillette, *King, Warrior, Magician, Lover: Rediscovering the Archetypes of the Mature Masculine* (San Francisco: HarperOne, 1991).

106 Marie Ellis, "Can You Die From a Broken Heart?" *Medical News Today* July 13, 2015. Accessed October 15, 2015 http://www.medicalnewstoday.com/articles/273268.php

107 Viktor Frankl, *Man's Search for Meaning* (New York City: Touchstone Books/ Simon & Schuster, 1984) p. 123.

108 Nancy Tilden, "The Opportunity in Conflict" Agile Learning Centers blog, November 9, 2014. Accessed September 21, 2015 http://nancy.agilelearningcenters.org/tag/mastery/

109 Deborah Frieze, "Two Loops Model" December 16, 2010. Accessed September 21, 2015 https://vimeo.com/17907928

110 Vanessa Reid, "Practicing Conscious Closure" June 14, 2011. http://deepeningcommunity.ca/blogs/vanessa-reid/practicing-conscious-closure

111 Peter Block, *The Answer to How is Yes: Acting on What Matters* (San Francisco: Berrett-Koehler, 2002) opening page.

112 From a personal interview conducted February 2015 for the Thrivable World Quest.

113 Vanessa Reid, personal Facebook post, March 20, 2015.

114 Donella Meadows, "Leverage Points: Places to Intervene in a System." Accessed April 15, 2016 http://donellameadows.org/archives/leverage-points-places-to-intervene-in-a-system/

115 Ian MacKenzie, *Dear Guardians: A Love Letter to the Temple Guardians of Burning Man* July 2014. Accessed September 19, 2014 http://www.ianmack.com/dear-guardians/

116 From a personal interview conducted January 2015 for the Thrivable World Quest.